ADJUSTMENTS

BLAKENEY	=	CROMER	+ 0:25
WEST STONES	=	HUNSTANTON	+ 0:10
WISBECK CUT	=	HUNSTANTON	+ 0:10
LAWYERS CREEK	=	HUNSTANTON	
CLEY	=	CROMER	- 0:10
MUNDESLEY	=	CROMER	+ 0:15

CW00522447

... listed are an average of the actual time differences.

Times quoted **within the following tables** have been compiled using variable time differences to give more accurate predictions. Times shown may therefore be different to those calculated using mean differences as quoted in other publications.

TELEPHONE NUMBERS

Norfolk Police	01603 768769
Suffolk Police	01473 613500
Walton Coast Guard	01255 675518
Yarmouth Coast Guard	01493 851338
Drug Smuggling Hotline	0800 595000
Weather (Marinecall Anglia)	0891 500455
Emergency inc Coast Guard	999 or Channel 16 VHF

Coastal Tourist Centres

Cromer	01263 512497
Hunstanton	01485 532610
King's Lynn	01553 763044
Sheringham	01263 824329
Wells next the Sea	01328 710885
Lowestoft	01502 523000
Felixstowe	01394 276770

JANUARY 2005

"NT" = No Tide

		Heights at CROMER				CROMER SHERINGHAM				KING'S LYNN QUAY				HUNSTANTON				BLAKENEY BAR			
		HIGH		LOW		HIGH WATER		LOW WATER		HIGH WATER		LOW WATER		HIGH WATER		LOW WATER		HIGH WATER		LOW WATER	
		AM	PM	AM	PM	AM	PM	AM	PM	AM	PM	AM	PM	AM	PM	AM	PM	AM	PM	AM	PM
1	SAT	4.2	4.5	1.1	1.6	10:01	22:04	4:22	16:31	9:53	21:56	5:47	17:52	9:39	21:42	4:05	16:10	9:52	21:55	3:50	15:51
2	SUN	4.1	4.4	1.2	1.7	10:45	22:49	5:07	17:16	10:35	22:39	6:18	18:24	10:20	22:23	4:42	16:47	10:35	22:40	4:32	16:39
3	MON	4.0	4.3	1.3	1.8	11:37	23:42	5:58	18:09	11:24	23:29	6:53	19:01	11:07	23:12	5:21	17:32	11:26	23:31	5:18	17:30
4	TUES		4.3	1.4	1.9	NT	12:36	6:57	19:12	NT	12:20	7:33	19:43	NT	12:01	6:08	18:23	NT	12:24	6:13	18:28
5	WED	4.0	3.9	1.4	1.9	0:45	13:43	8:04	20:26	0:28	13:23	8:18	20:37	0:09	13:03	7:03	19:21	0:32	13:28	7:16	19:30
6	THUR	4.3	4.1	1.4	1.7	1:54	14:45	9:08	21:33	1:35	14:29	9:34	22:07	1:15	14:11	8:11	20:40	1:40	14:32	8:20	20:47
7	FRI	4.3	4.2	1.4	1.5	3:04	15:48	10:09	22:34	2:49	15:36	10:59	23:35	2:32	15:20	9:28	22:01	2:51	15:37	9:28	21:56
8	SAT	4.5	4.5	1.2	1.1	4:11	16:44	11:07	23:31	4:00	16:35	NT	12:18	3:44	16:21	10:38	23:10	4:01	16:34	10:30	22:57
9	SUN	4.7	4.7	1.1		5:10	17:35	11:56	NT	5:02	17:29	0:53	13:29	4:48	17:16	11:43	NT	5:01	17:27	11:25	23:53
10	MON	4.8	5.0	0.8	0.8	6:04	18:24	0:21	12:44	5:59	18:20	2:05	14:36	5:47	18:08	0:16	12:43	5:56	18:17	NT	12:17
11	TUES	5.0	5.2	0.5	0.8	6:54	19:10	1:08	13:28	6:52	19:09	3:14	15:41	6:41	18:59	1:15	13:39	6:48	19:04	0:45	13:06
12	WED	5.0	5.3	0.3	0.7	7:43	19:58	1:58	14:19	7:43	19:57	4:08	16:22	7:32	19:46	2:09	14:26	7:39	19:53	1:36	13:56
13	THUR	5.0	5.2	0.2	0.8	8:34	20:47	2:52	15:11	8:31	20:43	4:44	16:57	8:19	20:31	2:51	15:06	8:28	20:40	2:26	14:43
14	FRI	4.9	5.1	0.3	1.0	9:23	21:34	3:43	16:00	9:18	21:28	5:20	17:32	9:05	21:14	3:34	15:47	9:16	21:27	3:14	15:30
15	SAT	4.7	4.9	0.5	1.2	10:13	22:24	4:36	16:51	10:05	22:15	5:56	18:06	9:50	22:00	4:15	16:26	10:05	22:15	4:02	16:16
16	SUN	4.4	4.6	0.8	1.4	11:05	23:16	5:27	17:43	10:54	23:04	6:32	18:43	10:38	22:48	4:58	17:10	10:55	23:05	4:51	17:05
17	MON	4.1		1.0	1.7	11:59	NT	6:22	18:38	11:45	23:54	7:09	19:20	11:28	23:36	5:41	17:53	11:47	23:57	5:41	17:55
18	TUES	4.2	3.9	1.4	2.0	0:09	12:59	7:20	19:41	NT	12:41	7:47	20:02	NT	12:22	6:27	18:44	NT	12:45	6:35	18:54
19	WED	4.1	3.8	1.7	2.1	1:12	14:03	8:26	20:51	0:53	13:45	8:37	21:10	0:34	13:26	7:21	19:50	0:57	13:49	7:36	20:02
20	THUR	3.9	3.8	1.9	2.1	2:19	15:08	9:27	21:55	2:02	14:53	10:00	22:39	1:43	14:36	8:34	21:10	2:06	14:55	8:41	21:12
21	FRI	3.9	3.9	1.9	2.0	3:27	16:05	10:24	22:53	3:14	15:54	11:20	23:58	2:57	15:38	9:47	22:20	3:16	15:55	9:44	22:14
22	SAT	3.9	4.0	1.8	1.7	4:27	16:55	11:16	23:41	4:17	16:47	NT	12:32	4:02	16:33	10:51	23:24	4:17	16:46	10:40	23:09
23	SUN	4.1	4.2	1.7		5:18	17:38	11:59	NT	5:11	17:32	1:08	13:32	4:57	17:19	11:46	NT	5:10	17:30	11:28	23:53
24	MON	4.2	4.4	1.5	1.5	6:01	18:14	0:21	12:34	5:56	18:10	2:05	14:24	5:44	17:58	0:16	12:33	5:53	18:07	NT	12:08
25	TUES	4.4	4.6	1.3	1.4	6:38	18:47	0:57	13:07	6:35	18:45	2:58	15:13	6:24	18:34	1:00	13:14	6:31	18:41	0:32	12:44
26	WED	4.5	4.7	1.1	1.3	7:12	19:19	1:28	13:38	7:11	19:19	3:41	15:53	7:01	19:09	1:39	13:53	7:06	19:14	1:06	13:18
27	THUR	4.5	4.8	1.1	1.2	7:47	19:53	2:04	14:15	7:46	19:52	4:12	16:19	7:35	19:41	2:15	14:22	7:42	19:48	1:43	13:52
28	FRI	4.6	4.9	0.8	1.2	8:21	20:27	2:41	14:51	8:19	20:24	4:37	16:43	8:07	20:12	2:44	14:50	8:16	20:21	2:17	14:25
29	SAT	4.5	4.9	0.8	1.2	8:56	21:03	3:18	15:26	8:52	20:58	5:03	17:09	8:39	20:45	3:13	15:21	8:50	20:56	2:50	14:59
30	SUN	4.5	4.8	0.8	1.4	9:33	21:39	3:57	16:04	9:27	21:32	5:29	17:35	9:14	21:18	3:44	15:51	9:25	21:31	3:27	15:34
31	MON	4.4	4.7	0.9	1.4	10:11	22:17	4:36	16:43	10:03	22:09	5:56	18:01	9:48	21:54	4:15	16:22	10:03	22:09	4:02	16:10

Times GMT

JANUARY 2005

"NT" = No Tide

Day	BURNHAM OVERY STAITHE HIGH WATER AM	PM	WELLS BAR HIGH WATER AM	PM	LOW WATER AM	PM	WELLS QUAY HIGH WATER AM	PM	LOW WATER AM	PM	HEMSBY HIGH WATER AM	PM	LOW WATER AM	PM	Gt.YARMOUTH BRITANNIA PIER HIGH WATER AM	PM	LOW WATER AM	PM	
1	10:14	22:17	9:43	21:46	3:36	15:43	10:04	22:07	5:24	17:30	10:56	22:59	5:17	17:26	23:03	12:10	6:05	18:01	---
2	10:55	22:58	10:25	22:29	4:17	16:24	10:45	22:48	6:02	18:08	11:40	23:44	6:02	18:11	23:38	12:59	6:49	18:44	---
3	11:42	23:47	11:14	23:19	5:02	17:13	11:32	23:37	6:43	18:53	NT	12:32	6:53	19:04	0:21	13:52	7:38	19:35	--
4	NT	12:36	NT	12:10	5:55	18:10	NT	12:26	7:31	19:46	0:37	13:31	7:52	20:07	1:12	14:52	8:35	20:37	--
5	0:44	13:38	0:18	13:13	6:56	19:16	0:34	13:28	8:27	20:46	1:40	14:38	8:59	21:21	2:15	15:53	9:36	21:47	-
6	1:50	14:46	1:25	14:19	8:02	20:29	1:40	14:36	9:36	22:04	2:49	15:40	10:03	22:28	3:27	16:53	10:40	23:00	-
7	3:07	15:55	2:39	15:26	9:11	21:40	2:57	15:45	10:50	23:22	3:59	16:43	11:04	23:29	4:46	17:51	11:44	NT	-
8	4:19	16:56	3:50	16:25	10:15	22:43	4:09	16:46	11:59	NT	5:06	17:39	NT	12:02	6:02	18:44	0:10	12:44	---
9	5:23	17:51	4:52	17:19	11:12	23:41	5:13	17:41	0:30	13:02	6:05	18:30	0:26	12:51	7:09	19:36	1:11	13:40	----
10	6:22	18:43	5:49	18:10	NT	12:06	6:12	18:33	1:34	14:01	6:59	19:19	1:16	13:39	8:10	20:25	2:08	14:32	-----
11	7:16	19:34	6:42	18:59	0:34	12:56	7:06	19:24	2:31	14:55	7:49	20:05	2:03	14:23	9:07	21:14	3:02	15:22	------
12	8:07	20:21	7:33	19:47	1:26	13:45	7:57	20:11	3:25	15:42	8:38	20:53	2:53	15:14	9:59	21:59	3:53	16:10	--------
13	8:54	21:06	8:21	20:33	2:14	14:31	8:44	20:56	4:08	16:24	9:29	21:42	3:47	16:06	10:49	22:43	4:42	16:56	--------
14	9:40	21:49	9:08	21:18	3:01	15:16	9:30	21:39	4:52	17:05	10:18	22:29	4:38	16:55	11:38	23:24	5:30	17:41	
15	10:25	22:35	9:55	22:05	3:48	16:01	10:15	22:25	5:35	17:46	11:08	23:19	5:31	17:46	NT	12:26	6:18	18:26	
16	11:13	23:23	10:44	22:54	4:35	16:49	11:03	23:13	6:18	18:31	NT	12:00	6:22	18:38	0:07	13:18	7:08	19:14	
17	NT	12:03	11:35	23:44	5:24	17:38	11:53	NT	7:03	19:16	0:11	12:54	7:17	19:33	0:52	14:11	8:00	20:05	--
18	0:11	12:57	NT	12:31	6:16	18:35	0:01	12:47	7:50	20:08	1:04	13:54	8:15	20:36	1:42	15:11	8:56	21:07	-
19	1:09	14:01	0:43	13:35	7:16	19:43	0:59	13:51	8:46	21:15	2:07	14:58	9:21	21:46	2:44	16:14	9:57	22:19	
20	2:18	15:11	1:52	14:43	8:23	20:55	2:08	15:01	9:58	22:33	3:14	16:03	10:22	22:50	3:56	17:12	11:01	23:29	
21	3:32	16:13	3:04	15:44	9:28	21:59	3:22	16:03	11:09	23:42	4:22	17:00	11:19	23:48	5:08	18:01	11:58	NT	
22	4:37	17:08	4:07	16:37	10:26	22:55	4:27	16:58	NT	12:12	5:22	17:50	NT	12:11	6:12	18:46	0:26	12:49	-
23	5:32	17:54	5:01	17:22	11:15	23:41	5:22	17:44	0:43	13:05	6:13	18:33	0:36	12:54	7:08	19:26	1:18	13:34	--
24	6:19	18:33	5:46	18:00	11:56	NT	6:09	18:23	1:34	13:50	6:56	19:09	1:16	13:29	7:55	20:01	2:02	14:14	---
25	6:59	19:09	6:25	18:35	0:21	12:33	6:49	18:59	2:17	14:30	7:33	19:42	1:52	14:02	8:37	20:36	2:40	14:50	----
26	7:36	19:44	7:01	19:09	0:56	13:08	7:26	19:34	2:55	15:08	8:07	20:14	2:23	14:33	9:16	21:09	3:17	15:25	----
27	8:10	20:16	7:36	19:42	1:32	13:41	8:00	20:06	3:30	15:38	8:42	20:48	2:59	15:10	9:53	21:42	3:53	15:58	-----
28	8:42	20:47	8:09	20:14	2:05	14:13	8:32	20:37	4:00	16:07	9:16	21:22	3:36	15:46	10:28	22:13	4:27	16:30	-----
29	9:14	21:20	8:42	20:48	2:38	14:46	9:04	21:10	4:31	16:38	9:51	21:57	4:13	16:21	11:03	22:46	5:02	17:03	-----
30	9:49	21:53	9:17	21:22	3:13	15:20	9:39	21:43	5:02	17:09	10:28	22:34	4:52	16:59	11:39	23:19	5:38	17:37	-----
31	10:23	22:29	9:53	21:59	3:48	15:55	10:13	22:19	5:35	17:41	11:06	23:12	5:31	17:38	NT	12:18	6:16	18:13	---

FEBRUARY 2005

"NT" = No Tide

		Heights at CROMER HIGH AM	HIGH PM	LOW AM	LOW PM	CROMER SHERINGHAM HIGH WATER AM	HW PM	LOW WATER AM	LW PM	KING'S LYNN QUAY HIGH WATER AM	HW PM	LOW WATER AM	LW PM	HUNSTANTON HIGH WATER AM	HW PM	LOW WATER AM	LW PM	BLAKENEY BAR HIGH WATER AM	HW PM	LOW WATER AM	LW PM

#	Day	Cromer HIGH AM	HIGH PM	LOW AM	LOW PM	C/S HW AM	HW PM	LW AM	LW PM	KL HW AM	HW PM	LW AM	LW PM	Hun HW AM	HW PM	LW AM	LW PM	Blk HW AM	HW PM	LW AM	LW PM
1	TUES	4.3	4.5	1.1	1.5	10:55	23:05	5:20	17:31	10:44	22:54	6:27	18:33	10:28	22:38	4:51	16:58	10:45	22:55	4:44	16:53
2	WED	4.1		1.3	1.7	11:45	NT	6:10	18:25	11:32	23:47	7:02	19:11	11:15	23:29	5:33	17:44	11:34	23:50	5:31	17:44
3	THUR	4.3	4.0	1.5	1.8	0:01	12:48	7:11	19:38	NT	12:31	7:42	20:00	NT	12:12	6:22	18:41	NT	12:35	6:27	18:51
4	FRI	4.2	3.9	1.7	1.8	1:16	14:04	8:30	21:01	0:57	13:46	8:42	21:23	0:37	13:27	7:25	20:00	1:02	13:50	7:40	20:12
5	SAT	4.1	4.1	1.7	1.6	2:37	15:21	9:43	22:17	2:21	15:07	10:22	23:09	2:03	14:50	8:54	21:36	2:24	15:09	8:58	21:35
6	SUN	4.3	4.3	1.5	1.2	3:58	16:28	10:52	23:22	3:46	16:18	11:57	NT	3:30	16:03	10:19	22:57	3:47	16:18	10:13	22:46
7	MON	4.5	4.7	1.3		5:03	17:24	11:48	NT	4:55	17:17	0:39	13:16	4:41	17:04	11:31	NT	4:54	17:15	11:16	23:46
8	TUES	4.7	5.0	1.0	0.8	5:59	18:14	0:15	12:35	5:54	18:10	1:55	14:25	5:42	17:58	0:06	12:34	5:51	18:07	NT	12:09
9	WED	4.9	5.2	0.5	0.8	6:47	18:58	1:00	13:18	6:45	18:57	3:04	15:29	6:34	18:46	1:07	13:29	6:41	18:53	0:37	12:56
10	THUR	5.1	5.4	0.2	0.6	7:31	19:42	1:44	14:03	7:31	19:42	3:58	16:11	7:21	19:31	1:59	14:14	7:26	19:38	1:24	13:42
11	FRI	5.1	5.4	0.1	0.6	8:16	20:27	2:35	14:51	8:14	20:24	4:33	16:43	8:02	20:12	2:38	14:50	8:11	20:21	2:10	14:25
12	SAT	5.0	5.3	0.2	0.8	8:59	21:10	3:20	15:35	8:55	21:05	5:04	17:14	8:42	20:52	3:15	15:26	8:53	21:03	2:53	15:06
13	SUN	4.8	5.0	0.4	1.0	9:42	21:52	4:07	16:19	9:35	21:45	5:35	17:45	9:21	21:31	3:50	16:02	9:34	21:44	3:35	15:47
14	MON	4.5	4.7	0.8	1.2	10:24	22:35	4:51	17:02	10:15	22:26	6:06	18:14	10:00	22:11	4:26	16:37	10:15	22:26	4:16	16:27
15	TUES	4.3	4.3	1.1	1.6	11:08	23:22	5:35	17:47	10:57	23:10	6:36	18:46	10:41	22:54	5:02	17:14	10:58	23:11	4:57	17:09
16	WED	4.0		1.5	1.9	11:57	NT	6:23	18:41	11:43	NT	7:10	19:22	11:26	23:43	5:42	17:56	11:45	NT	5:42	17:59
17	THUR	4.0	3.7	2.0	2.0	0:16	12:57	7:21	19:47	0:01	12:39	7:48	20:06	NT	12:20	6:28	18:50	0:04	12:43	6:36	19:00
18	FRI	3.7	3.6	2.2	2.0	1:26	14:12	8:35	21:11	1:07	13:54	8:48	21:37	0:47	13:35	7:30	20:14	1:12	13:58	7:45	20:23
19	SAT	3.7	3.7	2.2	2.1	2:52	15:30	9:53	22:27	2:36	15:17	10:34	23:24	2:18	15:00	9:04	21:50	2:39	15:19	9:08	21:47
20	SUN	3.7	3.9	2.1	1.9	4:09	16:34	10:57	23:24	3:58	16:24	NT	12:06	3:42	16:09	10:28	23:03	3:59	16:24	10:10	22:50
21	MON	3.9	4.1	1.9		5:06	17:19	11:44	NT	4:58	17:12	0:44	13:11	4:44	16:58	11:27	23:53	4:57	17:11	11:12	23:35
22	TUES	4.1	4.3	1.7	1.2	5:47	17:56	0:06	12:20	5:42	17:51	1:41	14:04	5:29	17:39	NT	12:15	5:40	17:48	11:52	NT
23	WED	4.4	4.6	1.4	1.3	6:23	18:28	0:40	12:51	6:19	18:25	2:31	14:47	6:07	18:13	0:39	12:54	6:16	18:22	0:13	12:26
24	THUR	4.5	4.8	0.9	1.2	6:54	18:59	1:10	13:21	6:52	18:58	3:17	15:33	6:41	18:47	1:17	13:32	6:48	18:54	0:47	12:59
25	FRI	4.7	4.9	0.7	1.1	7:25	19:29	1:40	13:52	7:25	19:29	3:55	16:03	7:15	19:19	1:55	14:03	7:20	19:24	1:20	13:30
26	SAT	4.8	5.1	0.6	1.0	7:56	20:01	2:15	14:25	7:55	20:00	4:19	16:27	7:44	19:49	2:22	14:32	7:51	19:56	1:52	14:02
27	SUN	4.8	5.1	1.2	1.0	8:29	20:35	2:51	15:00	8:26	20:32	4:43	16:50	8:14	20:20	2:50	14:59	8:23	20:29	2:25	14:34
28	MON	4.7	5.0	0.6	1.0	9:02	21:12	3:25	15:37	8:58	21:07	5:08	17:16	8:45	20:54	3:20	15:28	8:56	21:05	2:58	15:08

FEBRUARY 2005

"NT" = No Tide

BURNHAM OVERY STAITHE		WELLS BAR				WELLS QUAY				HEMSBY				Gt.YARMOUTH BRITANNIA PIER				
HIGH WATER		HIGH WATER		LOW WATER		HIGH WATER		LOW WATER		HIGH WATER		LOW WATER		HIGH WATER		LOW WATER		
AM	PM	AM	PM	AM	PM	AM	PM	AM	PM	AM	PM	AM	PM	AM	PM	AM	PM	
11:03	23:13	10:34	22:44	4:28	16:37	10:53	23:03	6:11	18:19	11:50	0:00	6:15	18:26	0:00	13:03	7:00	18:58	---
11:50	NT	11:22	23:37	5:14	17:27	11:40	23:54	6:54	19:06	NT	12:40	7:05	19:20	0:44	13:54	7:51	19:53	--
0:04	12:47	NT	12:21	6:09	18:32	NT	12:37	7:45	20:05	0:56	13:43	8:06	20:33	1:43	14:58	8:52	21:07	-
1:12	14:02	0:47	13:36	7:20	19:53	1:02	13:52	8:50	21:25	2:11	14:59	9:25	21:56	3:02	16:09	10:06	22:31	-
2:38	15:25	2:11	14:57	8:41	21:19	2:28	15:15	10:18	22:59	3:32	16:16	10:38	23:12	4:32	17:19	11:21	23:53	-
4:05	16:38	3:36	16:08	9:58	22:32	3:55	16:28	11:41	NT	4:53	17:23	11:47	NT	5:56	18:21	NT	12:29	--
5:16	17:39	4:45	17:07	11:02	23:33	5:06	17:29	0:18	12:50	5:58	18:19	0:17	12:43	7:07	19:18	1:00	13:29	----
6:17	18:33	5:44	18:00	11:57	NT	6:07	18:23	1:24	13:51	6:54	19:09	1:11	13:30	8:06	20:11	1:59	14:22	-----
7:09	19:21	6:35	18:47	0:26	12:46	6:59	19:11	2:23	14:45	7:42	19:53	1:55	14:13	8:59	20:59	2:52	15:10	------
7:56	20:06	7:21	19:32	1:14	13:31	7:46	19:56	3:14	15:29	8:26	20:37	2:39	14:58	9:46	21:44	3:40	15:55	--------
8:37	20:47	8:04	20:14	1:59	14:13	8:27	20:37	3:55	16:07	9:11	21:22	3:30	15:46	10:29	22:25	4:25	16:37	--------
9:17	21:27	8:45	20:55	2:40	14:53	9:07	21:17	4:32	16:44	9:54	22:05	4:15	16:30	11:10	23:04	5:07	17:16	--------
9:56	22:06	9:25	21:35	3:21	15:33	9:46	21:56	5:09	17:21	10:37	22:47	5:02	17:14	11:50	23:41	5:49	17:55	-----
10:35	22:46	10:05	22:16	4:01	16:12	10:25	22:36	5:46	17:57	11:19	23:30	5:46	17:57	NT	12:30	6:30	18:34	----
11:16	23:29	10:47	23:00	4:41	16:53	11:06	23:19	6:23	18:35	NT	12:03	6:30	18:42	0:20	13:12	7:14	19:18	--
NT	12:01	11:33	23:51	5:25	17:41	11:51	NT	7:04	19:18	0:17	12:52	7:18	19:53	1:05	14:03	8:03	20:12	-
0:18	12:55	NT	12:29	6:17	18:41	0:08	12:45	7:51	20:14	1:11	13:52	8:16	20:42	2:02	15:04	9:03	21:24	
1:22	14:10	0:57	13:44	7:25	20:05	1:12	14:00	8:55	21:39	2:21	15:07	9:30	22:06	3:20	16:17	10:16	22:50	
2:53	15:35	2:26	15:07	8:51	21:31	2:43	15:25	10:28	23:12	3:47	16:25	10:48	23:22	4:49	17:22	11:31	NT	
4:17	16:44	3:48	16:14	10:05	22:36	4:07	16:34	11:49	NT	5:04	17:29	11:52	NT	6:03	18:14	0:02	12:30	
5:19	17:33	4:48	17:02	10:58	23:22	5:09	17:23	0:23	12:46	6:01	18:14	0:19	12:39	6:58	18:57	0:58	13:16	-
6:04	18:14	5:32	17:41	11:40	NT	5:54	18:04	1:12	13:30	6:42	18:51	1:01	13:15	7:43	19:36	1:41	13:56	--
6:42	18:48	6:09	18:15	0:02	12:15	6:32	18:38	1:57	14:11	7:18	19:23	1:35	13:46	8:22	20:12	2:20	14:31	----
7:16	19:22	6:42	18:48	0:36	12:49	7:06	19:12	2:33	14:48	7:49	19:54	2:05	14:16	8:58	20:48	2:55	15:05	-----
7:50	19:54	7:15	19:19	1:10	13:20	7:40	19:44	3:10	15:19	8:20	20:24	2:35	14:47	9:31	21:20	3:30	15:37	-----
8:19	20:24	7:45	19:50	1:41	13:51	8:09	20:14	3:38	15:48	8:51	20:56	3:10	15:20	10:03	21:53	4:02	16:08	------
8:49	20:55	8:16	20:22	2:13	14:22	8:39	20:45	4:07	16:16	9:24	21:30	3:46	15:55	10:35	22:26	4:36	16:40	------
9:20	21:29	8:48	20:57	2:45	14:55	9:10	21:19	4:37	16:46	9:57	22:07	4:20	16:32	11:08	22:58	5:10	17:14	-----

MARCH 2005

"NT" = No Tide

		Heights at CROMER				CROMER SHERINGHAM				KING'S LYNN QUAY				HUNSTANTON				BLAKENEY BAR			
		HIGH		LOW		HIGH WATER		LOW WATER		HIGH WATER		LOW WATER		HIGH WATER		LOW WATER		HIGH WATER		LOW WATER	
		AM	PM	AM	PM	AM	PM	AM	PM	AM	PM	AM	PM	AM	PM	AM	PM	AM	PM	AM	PM
1	TUES	4.6	4.9	0.7	1.1	9:40	21:51	4:04	16:16	9:33	21:44	5:35	17:42	9:19	21:30	3:51	15:59	9:32	21:43	3:34	15:4
2	WED	4.5	4.6	1.0	1.3	10:20	22:38	4:46	17:01	10:11	22:28	6:04	18:14	9:56	22:13	4:25	16:36	10:11	22:28	4:13	16:2
3	THUR	4.3	4.3	1.3	1.5	11:08	23:35	5:36	17:56	10:57	23:22	6:37	18:51	10:41	23:05	5:03	17:19	10:58	23:24	4:58	17:1
4	FRI		4.0	1.6	1.7	NT	12:10	6:36	19:07	11:55	NT	7:18	19:39	11:37	NT	5:51	18:18	11:58	NT	5:53	18:2
5	SAT	4.1	3.9	1.9	1.8	0:53	13:35	7:59	20:44	0:35	13:15	8:14	20:59	0:16	12:55	6:58	19:39	0:39	13:20	7:11	19:5
6	SUN	3.9	4.0	2.0	1.6	2:26	15:01	9:27	22:07	2:09	14:46	10:00	22:57	1:50	14:28	8:34	21:26	2:13	14:49	8:41	21:2
7	MON	4.1	4.3	1.7	1.2	3:54	16:17	10:43	23:16	3:42	16:06	11:46	NT	3:26	15:51	10:10	22:51	3:43	16:06	10:05	22:4
8	TUES	4.4	4.7	1.4		5:00	17:14	11:40	NT	4:52	17:06	0:32	13:06	4:38	16:52	11:23	23:54	4:51	17:05	11:08	23:3
9	WED	4.7	5.0	1.1	0.4	5:50	18:01	0:07	12:25	5:45	17:56	1:42	14:10	5:32	17:44	NT	12:20	5:43	17:53	11:57	NT
10	THUR	4.9	5.3	1.4	1.3	6:33	18:43	0:48	13:05	6:30	18:41	2:44	15:10	6:19	18:30	0:51	13:12	6:26	18:37	0:23	12:4
11	FRI	5.1	5.3	0.2	0.6	7:13	19:22	1:28	13:42	7:12	19:22	3:41	15:57	7:02	19:12	1:39	13:57	7:07	19:17	1:06	13:2
12	SAT	5.1	5.3	0.1	0.5	7:52	20:02	2:10	14:25	7:51	20:01	4:15	16:27	7:40	19:50	2:17	14:32	7:47	19:57	1:47	14:0
13	SUN	5.1	5.2	0.2	0.6	8:30	20:41	2:52	15:05	8:27	20:38	4:44	16:54	8:15	20:26	2:51	15:04	8:24	20:35	2:26	14:3
14	MON	4.9	4.9	0.5	0.8	9:06	21:20	3:32	15:45	9:02	21:15	5:12	17:22	8:49	21:02	3:23	15:36	9:00	21:13	3:03	15:1
15	TUES	4.6	4.7	0.8	1.1	9:45	22:00	4:12	16:24	9:38	21:52	5:39	17:48	9:24	21:38	3:55	16:07	9:37	21:51	3:40	15:5
16	WED	4.3	4.3	1.2	1.4	10:22	22:41	4:51	17:05	10:13	22:31	6:06	18:17	9:58	22:16	4:26	16:40	10:13	22:31	4:16	16:3
17	THUR	4.1	3.9	1.6	1.8	11:03	23:29	5:32	17:51	10:52	23:17	6:34	18:49	10:36	23:00	4:59	17:18	10:53	23:19	4:54	17:1
18	FRI	3.8		2.0	2.1	11:55	NT	6:22	18:52	11:41	NT	7:09	19:31	11:24	NT	5:41	18:07	11:43	NT	5:41	18:1
19	SAT	3.6	3.6	2.3	2.3	0:37	13:12	7:35	20:27	0:21	12:53	7:57	20:38	0:02	12:34	6:38	19:22	0:25	12:57	6:48	19:3
20	SUN	3.5	3.5	2.4	2.1	2:16	14:45	9:12	21:55	1:58	14:29	9:39	22:39	1:39	14:11	8:15	21:10	2:02	14:32	8:24	21:1
21	MON	3.7	3.7	2.3	1.9	3:45	15:58	10:29	22:56	3:33	15:46	11:26	NT	3:17	15:30	9:52	22:27	3:34	15:47	9:49	22:19
22	TUES	3.9	4.0	2.0	1.5	4:42	16:48	11:19	23:39	4:33	16:39	0:05	12:35	4:18	16:25	10:54	23:22	4:33	16:38	10:43	23:07
23	WED	4.1	4.3	1.7		5:23	17:27	11:56	NT	5:16	17:20	1:05	13:29	5:02	17:07	11:43	NT	5:15	17:18	11:25	23:45
24	THUR	4.4	4.6	1.4	1.2	5:56	17:59	0:14	12:47	5:51	17:54	1:54	14:12	5:39	17:42	0:05	12:22	5:48	17:51	11:59	NT
25	FRI	4.7	4.9	1.1	1.1	6:27	18:31	0:44	12:56	6:24	18:28	2:36	14:57	6:12	18:17	0:43	12:59	6:21	18:24	0:17	12:31
26	SAT	4.8	5.1	0.6	0.9	6:57	19:02	1:12	13:25	6:55	19:01	3:22	15:38	6:44	18:51	1:23	13:36	6:51	18:56	0:51	13:03
27	SUN	4.9	5.1	0.5	0.8	8:29	20:37	2:51	15:02	8:26	20:34	4:43	16:52	8:14	20:22	2:50	15:01	8:23	20:31	2:25	14:36
28	MON	4.9	5.1	0.5	0.8	9:02	21:13	3:26	15:39	8:58	21:08	5:09	17:17	8:45	20:55	3:21	15:30	8:56	21:06	2:59	15:10
29	TUES	4.9	5.0	0.5	0.8	9:37	21:52	4:03	16:18	9:31	21:45	5:34	17:44	9:17	21:31	3:50	16:01	9:30	21:44	3:33	15:46
30	WED	4.7	4.8	0.7	0.9	10:15	22:35	4:43	17:00	10:07	22:26	6:01	18:13	9:52	22:11	4:22	16:35	10:07	22:26	4:10	16:25
31	THUR	4.6	4.5	1.0	1.1	10:58	23:25	5:26	17:48	10:47	23:13	6:31	18:46	10:31	22:57	4:57	17:15	10:48	23:14	4:50	17:10

Times GMT / BST

BURNHAM OVERY STAITHE		WELLS BAR				WELLS QUAY				HEMSBY				Gt.YARMOUTH BRITANNIA PIER				
HIGH WATER		HIGH WATER		LOW WATER		HIGH WATER		LOW WATER		HIGH WATER		LOW WATER		HIGH WATER		LOW WATER		
AM	PM	AM	PM	AM	PM	AM	PM	AM	PM	AM	PM	AM	PM	AM	PM	AM	PM	
9:54	22:05	9:23	21:34	3:20	15:30	9:44	21:55	5:09	17:18	10:35	22:46	4:59	17:11	11:43	23:40	5:47	17:50	-----
10:31	22:48	10:01	22:18	3:58	16:11	10:21	22:38	5:44	17:56	11:15	23:39	5:41	17:56	NT	12:23	6:28	18:34	----
11:16	23:40	10:47	23:12	4:42	17:00	11:06	23:30	6:24	18:41	NT	12:03	6:31	18:51	0:28	13:10	7:17	19:29	--
NT	12:12	11:45	NT	5:36	18:05	NT	12:02	7:14	19:41	0:30	13:05	7:31	20:02	1:30	14:11	8:20	20:46	
0:51	13:30	0:25	13:05	6:51	19:34	0:41	13:20	8:22	21:05	1:48	14:30	8:54	21:39	2:57	15:29	9:41	22:18	-
2:25	15:03	1:59	14:36	8:23	21:09	2:15	14:53	9:58	22:48	3:21	15:56	10:22	23:02	4:35	16:49	11:06	23:44	-
4:01	16:26	3:32	15:56	9:49	22:26	3:51	16:16	11:31	NT	4:49	17:12	11:38	NT	6:00	18:01	NT	12:20	--
5:13	17:27	4:42	16:56	10:54	23:23	5:03	17:17	0:12	12:42	5:55	18:09	0:11	12:35	7:05	19:01	0:52	13:19	----
6:07	18:19	5:35	17:46	11:45	NT	5:57	18:09	1:13	13:36	6:45	18:56	1:02	13:29	7:57	19:53	1:47	14:08	-----
6:54	19:05	6:20	18:31	0:12	12:31	6:44	18:55	2:08	14:28	7:28	19:38	1:43	14:00	8:43	20:41	2:35	14:54	--------
7:37	19:47	7:02	19:12	0:56	13:12	7:27	19:37	2:55	15:12	8:08	20:17	2:23	14:37	9:25	21:24	3:20	15:35	--------
8:15	20:25	7:41	19:51	1:36	13:51	8:05	20:15	3:33	15:48	8:47	20:57	3:05	15:20	10:03	22:02	4:01	16:13	------
8:50	21:01	8:17	20:28	2:14	14:27	8:40	20:51	4:08	16:21	9:25	21:36	3:47	16:00	10:39	22:38	4:39	16:49	------
9:24	21:37	8:52	21:05	2:50	15:03	9:14	21:27	4:41	16:54	10:01	22:15	4:27	16:40	11:13	23:14	5:16	17:24	-----
9:59	22:13	9:28	21:42	3:26	15:38	9:49	22:03	5:14	17:26	10:40	22:55	5:07	17:19	11:45	23:50	5:52	18:00	----
10:33	22:51	10:03	22:21	4:01	16:15	10:23	22:41	5:46	18:00	11:17	23:36	5:46	18:00	NT	12:19	6:30	18:39	----
11:11	23:35	10:42	23:07	4:38	16:57	11:01	23:25	6:20	18:39	11:58	NT	6:27	18:46	0:33	12:58	7:12	19:29	-
11:59	NT	11:31	NT	5:24	17:52	11:49	NT	7:03	19:29	0:24	12:50	7:17	19:47	1:30	13:51	8:07	20:40	
0:37	13:09	0:11	12:43	6:29	19:17	0:27	12:59	8:02	20:47	1:32	14:07	8:30	21:22	2:55	15:08	9:27	22:11	
2:14	14:46	1:48	14:19	8:06	20:55	2:04	14:36	9:40	22:33	3:11	15:40	10:07	22:50	4:34	16:27	10:55	23:31	
3:52	16:05	3:23	15:36	9:33	22:04	3:42	15:55	11:14	23:48	4:40	16:53	11:24	23:51	5:47	17:28	NT	12:00	
4:53	17:00	4:23	16:29	10:29	22:53	4:43	16:50	NT	12:15	5:37	17:43	NT	12:14	6:38	18:17	0:25	12:47	-
5:37	17:42	5:06	17:10	11:12	23:32	5:27	17:32	0:41	13:02	6:18	18:22	0:34	12:51	7:20	19:01	1:10	13:28	--
6:14	18:17	5:41	17:44	11:47	NT	6:04	18:07	1:23	13:40	6:51	18:54	1:09	13:22	7:56	19:40	1:49	14:03	----
6:47	18:52	6:14	18:18	0:06	12:20	6:37	18:42	2:01	14:16	7:22	19:26	1:39	13:51	8:30	20:19	2:25	14:37	----
7:19	19:26	6:45	18:51	0:40	12:53	7:09	19:16	2:38	14:52	7:52	19:57	2:07	14:20	9:03	20:56	3:00	15:11	--GMT
8:49	20:57	8:16	20:24	2:13	14:24	8:39	20:47	4:07	16:18	9:24	21:32	3:46	15:57	10:35	22:31	4:34	16:44	------ BST
9:20	21:30	8:48	20:58	2:46	14:57	9:10	21:20	4:38	16:48	9:57	22:08	4:21	16:34	11:07	23:08	5:08	17:18	-----
9:52	21:58	9:21	21:35	3:19	15:32	9:42	21:56	5:08	17:20	10:32	22:47	4:58	17:13	11:39	23:46	5:43	17:53	-----
10:27	22:46	9:57	22:16	3:55	16:10	10:17	22:36	5:41	17:55	11:10	23:30	5:38	17:55	NT	12:14	6:21	18:34	-----
11:06	23:32	10:37	23:03	4:34	16:54	10:56	23:22	6:17	18:36	11:53	NT	6:21	18:43	0:29	12:52	7:03	19:21	---

APRIL 2005

"NT" = No Tide

		Heights at CROMER				CROMER SHERINGHAM				KING'S LYNN QUAY				HUNSTANTON				BLAKENEY BAR			
		HIGH		LOW		HIGH WATER		LOW WATER		HIGH WATER		LOW WATER		HIGH WATER		LOW WATER		HIGH WATER		LOW WATER	
		AM	PM	AM	PM	AM	PM	AM	PM	AM	PM	AM	PM	AM	PM	AM	PM	AM	PM	AM	PM
1	FRI	4.3		1.4	1.4	11:49	NT	6:18	18:47	11:35	NT	7:06	19:27	11:18	23:53	5:37	18:02	11:37	NT	5:37	18:0
2	SAT	4.2	4.1	1.7	1.7	0:28	12:56	7:23	20:08	0:12	12:38	7:50	20:21	NT	12:19	6:30	19:07	0:16	12:42	6:38	19:2
3	SUN	3.9	3.9	2.0	1.7	1:54	14:19	8:49	21:34	1:35	14:02	9:08	22:11	1:15	13:43	7:48	20:45	1:40	14:06	8:00	20:5
4	MON	3.9	4.1	2.0	1.4	3:26	15:47	10:14	22:55	3:12	15:35	11:05	NT	2:55	15:19	9:33	22:26	3:14	15:36	9:33	22:1
5	TUES	4.1	4.3	1.8	1.1	4:46	16:57	11:25	23:54	4:37	16:49	0:03	12:46	4:23	16:35	11:04	23:41	4:36	16:48	10:51	23:2
6	WED	4.4	4.6		0.8	5:44	17:52	NT	12:19	5:38	17:47	1:26	14:00	5:25	17:34	NT	12:10	5:36	17:45	11:49	NT
7	THUR	4.7	4.9	1.2	1.1	6:29	18:37	0:42	12:59	6:26	18:34	2:34	15:03	6:15	18:23	0:41	13:06	6:22	18:30	0:15	12:3
8	FRI	4.9	5.1	0.5	0.8	7:09	19:17	1:21	13:37	7:08	19:16	3:33	15:52	6:58	19:06	1:32	13:52	7:03	19:11	0:59	13:1
9	SAT	5.0	5.2	0.3	0.7	7:47	19:57	2:02	14:20	7:46	19:56	4:11	16:23	7:35	19:45	2:13	14:27	7:42	19:52	1:41	13:5
10	SUN	5.1	5.1	0.3	0.7	8:24	20:36	2:44	15:01	8:22	20:33	4:40	16:51	8:10	20:21	2:47	15:00	8:19	20:30	2:20	14:3
11	MON	5.0	5.0	0.5	0.7	9:00	21:15	3:23	15:40	8:56	21:10	5:06	17:18	8:43	20:57	3:18	15:31	8:54	21:08	2:56	15:1
12	TUES	4.8	4.8	0.7	0.9	9:36	21:52	4:02	16:19	9:30	21:45	5:33	17:45	9:16	21:31	3:49	16:02	9:29	21:44	3:32	15:4
13	WED	4.6	4.5	1.0	1.1	10:11	22:31	4:40	16:58	10:03	22:22	5:59	18:11	9:48	22:07	4:19	16:33	10:03	22:22	4:07	16:2
14	THUR	4.4	4.2	1.4	1.4	10:47	23:11	5:17	17:38	10:37	23:00	6:24	18:39	10:21	22:44	4:48	17:05	10:38	23:01	4:41	17:0
15	FRI	4.1		1.7	1.7	11:27	NT	5:57	18:24	11:15	23:48	6:52	19:11	10:58	23:30	5:20	17:43	11:17	23:51	5:17	17:4
16	SAT	3.9	3.8	2.0	2.0	0:02	12:18	6:46	19:25	NT	12:02	7:26	19:51	11:44	NT	6:01	18:32	NT	12:05	6:04	18:4
17	SUN	3.7	3.7	2.3	2.2	1:11	13:26	7:56	20:45	0:52	13:07	8:12	21:03	0:33	12:47	6:55	19:44	0:56	13:12	7:07	19:5
18	MON	3.5	3.7	2.5	2.0	2:35	14:49	9:18	22:07	2:18	14:33	9:49	22:54	2:00	14:15	8:25	21:22	2:21	14:36	8:32	21:2
19	TUES	3.7	3.8	2.3	1.7	4:01	16:04	10:37	23:07	3:49	15:53	11:39	NT	3:33	15:37	10:04	22:42	3:50	15:54	9:59	22:3
20	WED	3.9	4.1	2.1	1.4	4:58	16:58	11:31	23:52	4:50	16:50	0:21	12:53	4:36	16:36	11:10	23:39	4:49	16:49	10:57	23:2
21	THUR	4.1	4.3		1.1	5:41	17:42	NT	12:11	5:35	17:36	1:24	13:50	5:22	17:23	NT	12:02	5:33	17:34	11:42	NT
22	FRI	4.4	4.6	1.5	1.2	6:17	18:19	0:31	12:46	6:13	18:15	2:17	14:39	6:01	18:03	0:26	12:45	6:10	18:12	0:03	12:1
23	SAT	4.6	4.9	0.8	1.1	6:49	18:56	1:03	13:17	6:47	18:54	3:08	15:28	6:36	18:43	1:10	13:28	6:43	18:50	0:40	12:5
24	SUN	4.8	5.0	0.6	0.9	7:22	19:30	1:36	13:53	7:22	19:30	3:51	16:04	7:12	19:20	1:51	14:04	7:17	19:25	1:16	13:3
25	MON	4.9	5.1	0.5	0.8	7:57	20:11	2:16	14:34	7:56	20:09	4:20	16:32	7:45	19:58	2:23	14:37	7:52	20:05	1:53	14:0
26	TUES	5.0	5.1	0.5	0.7	8:35	20:52	2:57	15:16	8:32	20:48	4:48	17:01	8:20	20:35	2:56	15:11	8:29	20:46	2:31	14:4
27	WED	4.9	4.9	0.6	0.7	9:14	21:37	3:39	16:00	9:09	21:31	5:17	17:32	8:56	21:17	3:30	15:47	9:07	21:30	3:10	15:3
28	THUR	4.8	4.7	0.8	0.8	9:59	22:26	4:24	16:50	9:51	22:17	5:48	18:05	9:37	22:02	4:07	16:25	9:50	22:17	3:52	16:1
29	FRI	4.7	4.4	1.1	1.1	10:46	23:23	5:14	17:44	10:36	23:11	6:22	18:43	10:20	22:55	4:45	17:11	10:37	23:12	4:37	17:0
30	SAT	4.4		1.4	1.3	11:41	NT	6:09	18:49	11:28	NT	7:01	19:28	11:11	23:57	5:32	18:04	11:30	NT	5:30	18:07

Times BST

APRIL 2005

"NT" = No Tide

Day	BURNHAM OVERY STAITHE HW AM	HW PM	WELLS BAR HW AM	HW PM	LW AM	LW PM	WELLS QUAY HW AM	HW PM	LW AM	LW PM	HEMSBY HW AM	HW PM	LW AM	LW PM	Gt.YARMOUTH BRITANNIA PIER HW AM	HW PM	LW AM	LW PM	
1	11:53	NT	11:25	NT	5:20	17:47	11:43	NT	6:59	19:24	0:20	12:44	7:13	19:42	1:23	13:38	7:54	20:23	--
2	0:28	12:54	0:02	12:28	6:19	19:00	0:18	12:44	7:53	20:31	1:23	13:51	8:18	21:03	2:35	14:41	9:01	21:47	-
3	1:50	14:18	1:25	13:52	7:41	20:32	1:40	14:08	9:13	22:08	2:49	15:14	9:44	22:29	4:12	16:02	10:29	23:16	-
4	3:30	15:54	3:02	15:25	9:16	22:03	3:20	15:44	10:55	23:47	4:21	16:42	11:09	23:50	5:45	17:25	11:56	NT	-
5	4:58	17:10	4:27	16:39	10:37	23:10	4:48	17:00	NT	12:24	5:41	17:52	NT	12:20	6:57	18:35	0:34	13:05	--
6	6:00	18:09	5:28	17:37	11:37	NT	5:50	17:59	1:00	13:29	6:39	18:47	0:49	13:14	7:51	19:37	1:35	14:00	----
7	6:50	18:58	6:16	18:24	0:04	12:25	6:40	18:48	1:59	14:22	7:24	19:32	1:37	13:54	8:38	20:29	2:27	14:47	-----
8	7:33	19:41	6:58	19:06	0:49	13:07	7:23	19:31	2:48	15:07	8:04	20:12	2:16	14:32	9:19	21:15	3:12	15:29	------
9	8:10	20:20	7:36	19:46	1:30	13:46	8:00	20:10	3:28	15:43	8:42	20:52	2:57	15:15	9:56	21:56	3:52	16:08	------
10	8:45	20:56	8:12	20:23	2:08	14:23	8:35	20:46	4:03	16:17	9:19	21:31	3:39	15:56	10:31	22:34	4:31	16:45	------
11	9:18	21:32	8:46	21:00	2:43	14:58	9:08	21:22	4:35	16:49	9:55	22:10	4:18	16:35	11:04	23:11	5:06	17:20	-----
12	9:51	22:06	9:20	21:35	3:18	15:33	9:41	21:56	5:07	17:21	10:31	22:47	4:57	17:14	11:35	23:47	5:42	17:55	-
13	10:23	22:42	9:53	22:12	3:52	16:08	10:13	22:32	5:38	17:53	11:06	23:26	5:35	17:53	NT	12:04	6:16	18:31	---
14	10:56	23:19	10:27	22:50	4:25	16:44	10:46	23:09	6:08	18:26	11:42	NT	6:12	18:33	0:25	12:34	6:50	19:11	--
15	11:33	NT	11:05	23:38	5:01	17:26	11:23	23:55	6:42	19:05	0:06	12:22	6:52	19:19	1:10	13:09	7:30	20:01	-
16	0:05	12:19	11:52	NT	5:46	18:21	NT	12:09	7:23	19:55	0:57	13:13	7:41	20:20	2:10	13:57	8:21	21:09	
17	1:08	13:22	0:42	12:57	6:48	19:37	0:58	13:12	8:20	21:09	2:06	14:21	8:51	21:40	3:35	15:03	9:35	22:28	
18	2:35	14:50	2:08	14:23	8:14	21:07	2:25	14:40	9:49	22:45	3:30	15:44	10:13	23:02	5:05	16:21	11:01	23:44	
19	4:08	16:12	3:39	15:43	9:43	22:17	3:58	16:02	11:25	NT	4:56	16:59	11:32	NT	6:15	17:29	NT	12:13	-
20	5:11	17:11	4:40	16:40	10:43	23:08	5:01	17:01	0:02	12:30	5:53	17:53	0:02	12:26	7:04	18:25	0:41	13:04	-
21	5:57	17:58	5:25	17:26	11:29	23:51	5:47	17:48	0:58	13:20	6:36	18:37	0:47	13:06	7:44	19:15	1:28	13:47	--
22	6:36	18:38	6:03	18:05	NT	12:08	6:26	18:28	1:44	14:03	7:12	19:14	1:26	13:41	8:20	20:01	2:10	14:26	----
23	7:11	19:18	6:37	18:44	0:29	12:45	7:01	19:08	2:26	14:44	7:44	19:51	1:58	14:12	8:55	20:46	2:49	15:04	-----
24	7:47	19:55	7:12	19:20	1:06	13:21	7:37	19:45	3:06	15:20	8:17	20:25	2:31	14:48	9:30	21:28	3:27	15:41	-----
25	8:20	20:33	7:46	19:59	1:42	13:58	8:10	20:23	3:39	15:54	8:52	21:00	3:11	15:29	10:05	22:11	4:05	16:19	------
26	8:55	21:10	8:22	20:38	2:19	14:36	8:45	21:00	4:13	16:29	9:30	21:47	3:52	16:11	10:40	22:52	4:43	16:59	------
27	9:31	21:52	8:59	21:21	2:57	15:16	9:21	21:42	4:48	17:05	10:09	22:32	4:34	16:55	11:16	23:39	5:22	17:41	-----
28	10:12	22:37	9:41	22:07	3:38	16:00	10:02	22:27	5:26	17:45	10:54	23:21	5:19	17:45	11:55	NT	6:05	18:28	----
29	10:55	23:30	10:26	23:01	4:22	16:50	10:45	23:20	6:06	18:32	11:41	NT	6:09	18:39	0:30	12:35	6:51	19:23	---
30	11:46	NT	11:18	NT	5:13	17:49	11:36	NT	6:53	19:26	0:18	12:36	7:04	19:44	1:32	13:23	7:45	20:28	--

MAY 2005

"NT" = No Tide

		Heights at CROMER				CROMER SHERINGHAM				KING'S LYNN QUAY				HUNSTANTON				BLAKENEY BAR			
		HIGH		LOW		HIGH WATER		LOW WATER		HIGH WATER		LOW WATER		HIGH WATER		LOW WATER		HIGH WATER		LOW WATER	
		AM	PM	AM	PM	AM	PM	AM	PM	AM	PM	AM	PM	AM	PM	AM	PM	AM	PM	AM	PM
1	SUN	4.1	4.2	1.8	1.4	0:32	12:52	7:20	20:10	0:16	12:34	7:47	20:22	NT	12:15	6:27	19:09	0:20	12:38	6:35	19:2
2	MON	4.0	4.1	2.0	1.5	1:57	14:11	8:45	21:29	1:38	13:53	9:00	22:02	1:19	13:34	7:40	20:36	1:42	13:57	7:54	20:4
3	TUES	4.0	4.1	2.0	1.4	3:16	15:27	9:59	22:36	3:02	15:14	10:44	23:37	2:45	14:57	9:14	22:03	3:04	15:16	9:16	21:5
4	WED	4.1	4.3	1.8	1.1	4:26	16:33	11:04	23:33	4:16	16:23	NT	12:14	4:01	16:08	10:35	23:12	4:16	16:23	10:27	22:5
5	THUR	4.4	4.5	1.5		5:20	17:27	11:55	NT	5:13	17:20	0:55	13:27	4:59	17:07	11:42	NT	5:12	17:18	11:24	23:5
6	FRI	4.6	4.7	1.3	1.1	6:06	18:12	0:20	12:37	6:01	18:08	2:01	14:27	5:49	17:56	0:11	12:36	5:58	18:05	NT	12:1
7	SAT	4.7	4.9	0.7	1.1	6:43	18:53	0:58	13:13	6:41	18:51	2:59	15:23	6:30	18:40	1:01	13:24	6:37	18:47	0:33	12:5
8	SUN	4.9	4.9	0.6	0.9	7:19	19:30	1:33	13:52	7:19	19:30	3:48	16:03	7:09	19:20	1:48	14:03	7:14	19:25	1:13	13:3
9	MON	4.9	4.9	0.7	0.8	7:55	20:10	2:13	14:33	7:54	20:08	4:18	16:31	7:43	19:57	2:20	14:36	7:50	20:04	1:50	14:0
10	TUES	4.8	4.8	0.8	0.9	8:31	20:48	2:53	15:12	8:28	20:44	4:45	16:58	8:16	20:32	2:52	15:07	8:25	20:41	2:27	14:4
11	WED	4.7	4.6	1.0	1.0	9:05	21:27	3:31	15:51	9:01	21:21	5:11	17:25	8:48	21:08	3:22	15:38	8:59	21:19	3:02	15:2
12	THUR	4.6	4.4	1.2	1.1	9:42	22:08	4:09	16:32	9:35	22:00	5:37	17:53	9:21	21:46	3:52	16:11	9:34	21:59	3:37	15:5
13	FRI	4.4	4.1	1.4	1.4	10:21	22:51	4:49	17:15	10:12	22:41	6:04	18:23	9:57	22:25	4:24	16:46	10:12	22:42	4:14	16:3
14	SAT	4.2	3.9	1.7	1.5	11:02	23:43	5:31	18:04	10:51	23:30	6:33	18:57	10:35	23:13	4:58	17:27	10:52	23:32	4:53	17:2
15	SUN	4.1		2.0	1.7	11:51	NT	6:21	19:02	11:37	NT	7:08	19:35	11:20	NT	5:40	18:13	11:39	NT	5:40	18:1
16	MON	3.8	3.9	2.2	1.8	0:44	12:51	7:21	20:01	0:27	12:33	7:48	20:23	0:08	12:14	6:28	19:10	0:31	12:37	6:36	19:2
17	TUES	3.7	3.9	2.3	3.8	1:57	13:59	8:36	21:18	1:38	13:40	8:49	21:46	1:19	13:21	7:31	20:21	1:42	13:44	7:46	20:3
18	WED	3.7	3.9	2.3	1.7	3:03	15:04	9:39	22:15	2:48	14:49	10:17	23:06	2:30	14:32	8:50	21:34	2:51	14:51	8:54	21:3
19	THUR	3.9	4.1	2.1	1.4	4:03	16:03	10:35	23:06	3:51	15:51	11:36	NT	3:35	15:35	10:02	22:37	3:52	15:52	9:57	22:2
20	FRI	4.1	4.3	1.8	1.2	4:52	16:55	11:24	23:50	4:43	16:46	0:17	12:44	4:29	16:32	11:03	23:33	4:42	16:45	10:50	23:17
21	SAT	4.3	4.5		1.0	5:34	17:39	NT	12:07	5:28	17:33	1:19	13:42	5:15	17:20	11:54	NT	5:26	17:31	11:36	0:00
22	SUN	4.5	4.7	1.2	1.0	6:12	18:22	0:28	12:45	6:08	18:18	2:14	14:37	5:56	18:06	0:23	12:44	6:05	18:15	NT	12:18
23	MON	4.7	4.9	0.8	1.0	6:50	19:04	1:05	13:22	6:48	19:03	3:10	15:34	6:37	18:53	1:12	13:33	6:44	18:58	0:42	13:00
24	TUES	4.9	5.0	0.7	0.8	7:29	19:49	1:43	14:06	7:29	19:48	3:58	16:14	7:19	19:37	1:58	14:17	7:24	19:44	1:23	13:45
25	WED	5.0	5.0	0.6	0.8	8:13	20:38	2:33	14:57	8:11	20:35	4:31	16:48	8:00	20:23	2:36	14:56	8:07	20:32	2:08	14:31
26	THUR	5.0	4.9	0.8	0.6	8:58	21:29	3:21	15:50	8:54	21:23	5:05	17:24	8:41	21:10	3:16	15:37	8:52	21:21	2:54	15:19
27	FRI	4.9	4.7	0.9	0.7	9:47	22:25	4:12	16:44	9:40	22:16	5:39	18:02	9:26	22:01	3:55	16:23	9:39	22:16	3:40	16:11
28	SAT	4.8	4.5	1.2	0.8	10:40	23:24	5:07	17:44	10:30	23:12	6:18	18:43	10:15	22:56	4:42	17:11	10:30	23:13	4:32	17:06
29	SUN	4.6		1.4	1.1	11:38	NT	6:06	18:49	11:25	NT	6:59	19:28	11:08	23:56	5:29	18:04	11:27	NT	5:27	18:07
30	MON	4.4	4.3	1.7	1.2	0:31	12:44	7:13	20:04	0:15	12:27	7:44	20:18	NT	12:08	6:24	19:03	0:19	12:31	6:29	19:16
31	TUES	4.1	4.3	1.9	1.3	1:47	13:55	8:31	21:11	1:27	13:36	8:43	21:37	1:07	13:16	7:26	20:14	1:32	13:41	7:41	20:23

Times BST

MAY 2005

"NT" = No Tide

	BURNHAM OVERY STAITHE HIGH WATER		WELLS BAR HIGH WATER		WELLS BAR LOW WATER		WELLS QUAY HIGH WATER		WELLS QUAY LOW WATER		HEMSBY HIGH WATER		HEMSBY LOW WATER		Gt.YARMOUTH BRITANNIA PIER HIGH WATER		Gt.YARMOUTH BRITANNIA PIER LOW WATER		
	AM	PM	AM	PM	AM	PM	AM	PM	AM	PM	AM	PM	AM	PM	AM	PM	AM	PM	
1	0:32	12:50	0:06	12:24	6:16	19:02	0:22	12:40	7:50	20:33	1:27	13:47	8:15	21:05	2:49	14:25	8:53	21:47	--
2	1:54	14:09	1:28	13:43	7:35	20:25	1:44	13:59	9:06	22:00	2:52	15:06	9:40	22:24	4:17	15:40	10:15	23:04	--
3	3:20	15:32	2:52	15:04	8:59	21:42	3:10	15:22	10:37	23:24	4:11	16:22	10:54	23:31	5:35	16:57	11:34	NT	--
4	4:36	16:43	4:06	16:13	10:12	22:45	4:26	16:33	11:56	NT	5:21	17:28	11:59	NT	6:37	18:07	0:13	12:40	--
5	5:34	17:42	5:03	17:10	11:11	23:38	5:24	17:32	0:32	13:01	6:15	18:22	0:28	12:50	7:28	19:08	1:11	13:35	---
6	6:24	18:31	5:51	17:58	11:59	NT	6:14	18:21	1:30	13:53	7:01	19:07	1:15	13:32	8:12	20:01	2:01	14:21	----
7	7:05	19:15	6:31	18:41	0:22	12:41	6:55	19:05	2:18	14:39	7:38	19:48	1:53	14:08	8:50	20:47	2:44	15:03	-----
8	7:44	19:55	7:09	19:20	1:03	13:20	7:34	19:45	3:03	15:19	8:14	20:25	2:28	14:47	9:26	21:29	3:24	15:42	-----
9	8:18	20:32	7:44	19:58	1:39	13:57	8:08	20:22	3:36	15:53	8:50	21:05	3:08	15:28	10:00	22:08	4:01	16:19	-----
10	8:51	21:07	8:18	20:34	2:15	14:32	8:41	20:57	4:09	16:25	9:26	21:43	3:48	16:07	10:31	22:46	4:37	16:55	-----
11	9:23	21:43	8:51	21:11	2:49	15:07	9:13	21:33	4:40	16:57	10:00	22:22	4:26	16:46	11:01	23:25	5:11	17:31	----
12	9:56	22:21	9:25	21:50	3:23	15:44	9:46	22:11	5:11	17:31	10:37	23:03	5:04	17:27	11:31	NT	5:45	18:10	---
13	10:32	23:00	10:02	22:31	3:59	16:23	10:22	22:50	5:44	18:07	11:16	23:46	5:44	18:10	0:08	12:03	6:22	18:53	--
14	11:10	23:48	10:41	23:20	4:37	17:08	11:00	23:38	6:19	18:48	11:57	NT	6:26	18:59	0:56	12:38	7:01	19:43	-
15	11:55	NT	11:27	NT	5:23	18:00	11:45	NT	7:02	19:36	0:38	12:46	7:16	19:57	1:56	13:22	7:49	20:41	-
16	0:43	12:49	0:17	12:23	6:17	19:03	0:33	12:39	7:51	20:34	1:39	13:46	8:16	21:06	3:05	14:16	8:49	21:47	-
17	1:54	13:56	1:28	13:30	7:26	20:12	1:44	13:46	8:56	21:46	2:52	14:54	9:31	22:13	4:21	15:19	10:00	22:50	
18	3:05	15:07	2:38	14:39	8:37	21:17	2:55	14:57	10:14	22:56	3:58	15:59	10:34	23:10	5:23	16:24	11:07	23:48	-
19	4:10	16:10	3:41	15:41	9:41	22:14	4:00	16:00	11:23	23:58	4:58	16:58	11:30	NT	6:15	17:27	NT	12:07	
20	5:04	17:07	4:33	16:36	10:36	23:04	4:54	16:57	NT	12:23	5:47	17:50	0:01	12:19	6:59	18:27	0:39	12:58	--
21	5:50	17:55	5:18	17:23	11:23	23:48	5:40	17:45	0:53	13:13	6:29	18:34	0:45	13:02	7:39	19:22	1:28	13:45	---
22	6:31	18:41	5:58	18:08	NT	12:07	6:21	18:31	1:42	14:02	7:07	19:17	1:23	13:40	8:18	20:14	2:11	14:29	----
23	7:12	19:28	6:38	18:53	0:31	12:50	7:02	19:18	2:28	14:49	7:45	19:59	2:00	14:17	8:57	21:04	2:55	15:13	-----
24	7:54	20:12	7:19	19:38	1:13	13:34	7:44	20:02	3:13	15:32	8:24	20:44	2:38	15:01	9:37	21:55	3:38	15:59	-----
25	8:35	20:58	8:01	20:25	1:57	14:19	8:25	20:48	3:53	16:13	9:08	21:33	3:28	15:52	10:18	22:45	4:22	16:46	-----
26	9:16	21:45	8:44	21:13	2:41	15:06	9:06	21:35	4:33	16:56	9:53	22:24	4:16	16:45	10:58	23:37	5:07	17:34	----
27	10:01	22:36	9:30	22:06	3:26	15:56	9:51	22:26	5:14	17:42	10:42	23:20	5:07	17:39	11:41	NT	5:54	18:27	----
28	10:50	23:31	10:20	23:02	4:17	16:50	10:40	23:21	6:02	18:32	11:35	NT	6:02	18:39	0:35	12:26	6:45	19:24	---
29	11:43	NT	11:15	NT	5:10	17:49	11:33	NT	6:50	19:26	0:19	12:33	7:01	19:44	1:37	13:15	7:39	20:26	--
30	0:31	12:43	0:05	12:17	6:11	18:56	0:21	12:33	7:47	20:27	1:26	13:39	8:08	20:59	2:47	14:14	8:43	21:35	
31	1:42	13:51	1:17	13:26	7:21	20:05	1:32	13:41	8:51	21:39	2:42	14:50	9:26	22:06	4:01	15:20	9:54	22:42	--

JUNE 2005

"NT" = No Tide

		Heights at CROMER				CROMER SHERINGHAM				KING'S LYNN QUAY				HUNSTANTON				BLAKENEY BAR			
		HIGH		LOW		HIGH WATER		LOW WATER		HIGH WATER		LOW WATER		HIGH WATER		LOW WATER		HIGH WATER		LOW WATER	
		AM	PM	AM	PM	AM	PM	AM	PM	AM	PM	AM	PM	AM	PM	AM	PM	AM	PM	AM	PM
1	WED	4.1	4.3	1.9	1.3	2:54	15:00	9:34	22:09	2:38	14:45	10:11	22:59	2:20	14:27	8:45	21:28	2:41	14:48	8:50	21:28
2	THUR	4.1	4.3	1.8	1.2	3:54	16:02	10:34	23:04	3:42	15:50	11:32	NT	3:26	15:34	9:57	22:35	3:43	15:51	9:54	22:27
3	FRI	4.3	4.4	1.7	1.1	4:48	16:57	11:26	23:52	4:39	16:49	0:14	12:47	4:25	16:35	11:05	23:35	4:38	16:48	10:52	23:19
4	SAT	4.4	4.5		1.1	5:35	17:45	NT	12:11	5:29	17:39	1:21	13:50	5:16	17:26	NT	12:02	5:27	17:37	11:42	NT
5	SUN	4.5	4.5	1.3	1.3	6:15	18:28	0:31	12:49	6:11	18:25	2:17	14:45	5:59	18:13	0:26	12:52	6:08	18:22	0:03	12:24
6	MON	4.6	4.6	1.1	1.2	6:54	19:08	1:08	13:27	6:52	19:07	3:14	15:40	6:41	18:57	1:15	13:38	6:48	19:02	0:45	13:05
7	TUES	4.6	4.6	1.1	1.1	7:29	19:48	1:43	14:09	7:29	19:47	3:58	16:14	7:19	19:36	1:58	14:16	7:24	19:43	1:23	13:46
8	WED	4.7	4.5	1.1	1.1	8:06	20:28	2:25	14:50	8:05	20:25	4:27	16:43	7:54	20:13	2:32	14:49	8:01	20:22	2:02	14:24
9	THUR	4.6	4.5	1.2	1.1	8:43	21:10	3:04	15:32	8:40	21:05	4:53	17:12	8:28	20:52	3:03	15:23	8:37	21:03	2:38	15:03
10	FRI	4.5	4.3	1.4	1.1	9:22	21:52	3:48	16:15	9:17	21:45	5:22	17:42	9:04	21:31	3:35	15:58	9:15	21:44	3:17	15:43
11	SAT	4.5	4.2	1.5	1.2	10:02	22:35	4:27	16:58	9:54	22:26	5:51	18:11	9:40	22:11	4:10	16:33	9:53	22:26	3:55	16:23
12	SUN	4.4	4.1	1.7	1.4	10:42	23:20	5:09	17:43	10:32	23:08	6:20	18:43	10:17	22:52	4:44	17:10	10:32	23:09	4:34	17:05
13	MON	4.3		1.8	1.4	11:25	NT	5:55	18:34	11:13	23:57	6:50	19:17	10:57	23:39	5:18	17:49	11:14	0:00	5:15	17:51
14	TUES	4.2	3.9	2.0	1.5	0:12	12:14	6:45	19:28	11:59	NT	7:25	19:53	11:41	NT	6:00	18:35	NT	12:02	6:03	18:43
15	WED	3.9	4.0	2.0	1.6	1:07	13:10	7:42	20:29	0:49	12:51	8:03	20:41	0:30	12:32	6:45	19:24	0:53	12:55	6:55	19:39
16	THUR	3.9	4.1	2.1	1.6	2:05	14:08	8:45	21:22	1:47	13:50	9:00	21:53	1:28	13:31	7:40	20:29	1:51	13:54	7:54	20:36
17	FRI	4.0	4.1	2.0	1.4	3:03	15:07	9:40	22:15	2:48	14:52	10:18	23:06	2:30	14:35	8:51	21:34	2:51	14:54	8:55	21:34
18	SAT	4.0	4.3	1.9	1.3	3:57	16:06	10:34	23:08	3:45	15:55	11:35	NT	3:29	15:39	10:01	22:39	3:46	15:56	9:56	22:31
19	SUN	4.2	4.5	1.6	1.1	4:50	17:02	11:27	23:54	4:41	16:54	0:19	12:48	4:27	16:40	11:06	23:41	4:40	16:53	10:53	23:23
20	MON	4.4	4.6		1.0	5:37	17:55	NT	12:16	5:31	17:50	1:26	13:56	5:18	17:38	NT	12:07	5:29	17:47	11:47	NT
21	TUES	4.7	4.8	1.1	1.0	6:25	18:46	0:41	13:02	6:21	18:44	2:32	15:07	6:09	18:33	0:40	13:09	6:18	18:40	0:14	12:39
22	WED	4.9	4.9	0.9	0.8	7:10	19:36	1:25	13:51	7:09	19:36	3:38	16:02	6:59	19:26	1:36	14:02	7:04	19:31	1:03	13:29
23	THUR	5.0	4.9	0.8	0.5	7:57	20:30	2:16	14:48	7:56	20:27	4:20	16:41	7:45	20:15	2:23	14:47	7:52	20:24	1:53	14:22
24	FRI	5.1	4.9	0.8	0.5	8:48	21:25	3:11	15:42	8:44	21:19	4:57	17:19	8:32	21:06	3:06	15:33	8:41	21:17	2:43	15:13
25	SAT	5.1	4.8	0.9	0.5	9:40	22:20	4:04	16:39	9:33	22:11	5:35	17:58	9:19	21:56	3:51	16:18	9:32	22:11	3:34	16:06
26	SUN	5.0	4.6	1.1	0.5	10:31	23:15	4:59	17:37	10:22	23:06	6:12	18:38	10:07	22:47	4:34	17:04	10:22	23:04	4:24	16:59
27	MON	4.9		1.4	1.0	11:25	NT	5:55	18:36	11:13	23:58	6:50	19:18	10:57	23:40	5:18	17:51	11:14	NT	5:15	17:53
28	TUES	4.5	4.5	1.4	1.0	0:13	12:23	6:53	19:38	NT	12:07	7:32	20:00	11:49	NT	6:08	18:41	0:01	12:10	6:11	18:51
29	WED	4.3	4.5	1.7	1.2	1:16	13:25	7:59	20:41	0:57	13:06	8:14	20:55	0:37	12:46	6:58	19:36	1:02	13:11	7:11	19:50
30	THUR	4.1	4.3	1.8	1.4	2:17	14:26	9:01	21:35	1:59	14:09	9:23	22:12	1:40	13:50	8:00	20:46	2:03	14:13	8:12	20:51

JUNE 2005

"NT" = No Tide

	BURNHAM OVERY STAITHE		WELLS BAR				WELLS QUAY				HEMSBY				Gt.YARMOUTH BRITANNIA PIER				
	HIGH WATER		HIGH WATER		LOW WATER		HIGH WATER		LOW WATER		HIGH WATER		LOW WATER		HIGH WATER		LOW WATER		
	AM	PM	AM	PM	AM	PM	AM	PM	AM	PM	AM	PM	AM	PM	AM	PM	AM	PM	
1	2:55	15:02	2:28	14:35	8:32	21:11	2:45	14:52	10:08	22:50	3:49	15:55	10:29	23:04	5:08	16:28	11:03	23:43	--
2	4:01	16:09	3:32	15:40	9:38	22:12	3:51	15:59	11:19	23:56	4:49	16:57	11:29	23:59	6:05	17:35	NT	12:06	--
3	5:00	17:10	4:29	16:39	10:38	23:06	4:50	17:00	NT	12:25	5:43	17:52	NT	12:21	6:56	18:37	0:40	13:03	---
4	5:51	18:01	5:19	17:29	11:29	23:51	5:41	17:51	0:55	13:20	6:30	18:40	0:47	13:06	7:40	19:30	1:30	13:52	---
5	6:34	18:48	6:01	18:15	NT	12:13	6:24	18:38	1:44	14:09	7:10	19:23	1:26	13:44	8:19	20:20	2:14	14:36	---
6	7:16	19:32	6:42	18:57	0:34	12:55	7:06	19:22	2:31	14:54	7:49	20:03	2:03	14:22	8:56	21:05	2:56	15:18	---
7	7:54	20:11	7:19	19:37	1:13	13:35	7:44	20:01	3:13	15:32	8:24	20:43	2:38	15:04	9:30	21:48	3:35	15:57	----
8	8:29	20:48	7:55	20:15	1:51	14:12	8:19	20:38	3:48	16:06	9:01	21:23	3:20	15:45	10:03	22:29	4:12	16:35	---
9	9:03	21:27	8:30	20:55	2:26	14:50	8:53	21:17	4:20	16:41	9:38	22:05	3:59	16:27	10:35	23:12	4:47	17:15	---
10	9:39	22:06	9:07	21:35	3:04	15:29	9:29	21:56	4:54	17:17	10:17	22:47	4:43	17:10	11:08	23:55	5:24	17:55	---
11	10:15	22:46	9:44	22:16	3:41	16:08	10:05	22:36	5:29	17:53	10:57	23:30	5:22	17:53	11:41	NT	6:01	18:37	--
12	10:52	23:27	10:22	22:58	4:19	16:49	10:42	23:17	6:04	18:31	11:37	NT	6:04	18:38	0:41	12:15	6:38	19:20	-
13	11:32	NT	11:03	23:47	4:59	17:34	11:22	NT	6:40	19:12	0:15	12:20	6:50	19:29	1:30	12:53	7:19	20:09	--
14	0:14	12:16	11:49	NT	5:45	18:24	0:04	12:06	7:22	19:58	1:07	13:09	7:40	20:23	2:25	13:38	8:07	21:01	--
15	1:05	13:07	0:39	12:41	6:36	19:19	0:55	12:57	8:09	20:49	2:02	14:05	8:37	21:24	3:22	14:29	9:00	21:57	-
16	2:03	14:06	1:37	13:40	7:35	20:18	1:53	13:56	9:06	21:53	3:00	15:03	9:40	22:17	4:21	15:29	10:02	22:54	--
17	3:05	15:10	2:38	14:42	8:38	21:17	2:55	15:00	10:15	22:56	3:58	16:02	10:35	23:10	5:17	16:34	11:05	23:50	--
18	4:04	16:14	3:35	15:45	9:40	22:16	3:54	16:04	11:22	0:00	4:52	17:01	11:29	NT	6:08	17:42	NT	12:07	--
19	5:02	17:15	4:31	16:44	10:39	23:10	4:52	17:05	NT	12:26	5:45	17:57	0:03	12:22	6:56	18:48	0:45	13:05	---
20	5:53	18:13	5:21	17:40	11:34	NT	5:43	18:03	1:00	13:25	6:32	18:50	0:49	13:11	7:42	19:51	1:37	14:00	----
21	6:44	19:08	6:11	18:34	0:03	12:28	6:34	18:58	1:58	14:25	7:20	19:41	1:36	13:57	8:30	20:51	2:30	14:54	-----
22	7:34	20:01	6:59	19:26	0:53	13:19	7:24	19:51	2:52	15:18	8:05	20:31	2:20	14:46	9:15	21:47	3:20	15:46	-----
23	8:20	20:50	7:46	20:17	1:42	14:10	8:10	20:40	3:39	16:04	8:52	21:25	3:11	15:43	10:01	22:42	4:08	16:38	-----
24	9:07	21:41	8:34	21:09	2:31	15:00	8:57	21:31	4:24	16:51	9:43	22:20	4:06	16:37	10:47	23:36	4:58	17:29	-----
25	9:54	22:31	9:23	22:01	3:20	15:51	9:44	22:21	5:09	17:37	10:35	23:15	4:59	17:34	11:33	NT	5:46	18:22	-----
26	10:42	23:22	10:12	22:53	4:09	16:43	10:32	23:12	5:54	18:25	11:26	NT	5:54	18:32	0:31	12:18	6:36	19:15	----
27	11:32	NT	11:03	23:48	4:59	17:36	11:22	NT	6:40	19:14	0:10	12:20	6:50	19:31	1:26	13:05	7:26	20:10	---
28	0:15	12:24	11:57	NT	5:53	18:32	0:05	12:14	7:30	20:05	1:08	13:18	7:48	20:33	2:24	13:56	8:20	21:08	---
29	1:12	13:21	0:47	12:56	6:51	19:31	1:02	13:11	8:22	21:02	2:11	14:20	8:54	21:36	3:26	14:53	9:20	22:08	---
30	2:15	14:25	1:49	13:59	7:53	20:33	2:05	14:15	9:25	22:09	3:12	15:21	9:56	22:30	4:28	15:56	10:24	23:09	--

JULY 2005

"NT" = No Tide

		Heights at CROMER				CROMER SHERINGHAM				KING'S LYNN QUAY				HUNSTANTON				BLAKENEY BAR			
	Times BST	HIGH		LOW		HIGH WATER		LOW WATER		HIGH WATER		LOW WATER		HIGH WATER		LOW WATER		HIGH WATER		LOW WATER	
		AM	PM	AM	PM	AM	PM	AM	PM	AM	PM	AM	PM	AM	PM	AM	PM	AM	PM	AM	PM
1	FRI	4.1	4.2	1.9	1.5	3:15	15:27	9:58	22:30	3:01	15:13	10:43	23:27	2:44	14:56	9:13	21:53	3:03	15:15	9:15	21:50
2	SAT	4.1	4.1	1.8	1.5	4:13	16:26	10:53	23:22	4:02	16:16	NT	12:01	3:47	16:01	10:24	22:57	4:02	16:16	10:16	22:46
3	SUN	4.1	4.2	1.7		5:04	17:21	11:45	NT	4:56	17:14	0:39	13:13	4:42	17:00	11:28	23:58	4:55	17:13	11:13	23:33
4	MON	4.2	4.3	1.6	1.4	5:51	18:09	0:07	12:31	5:46	18:05	1:45	14:17	5:33	17:53	NT	12:26	5:44	18:02	NT	12:03
5	TUES	4.3	4.3	1.5	1.4	6:33	18:53	0:49	13:10	6:30	18:51	2:42	15:17	6:19	18:40	0:48	13:17	6:26	18:47	0:22	12:47
6	WED	4.4	4.3	1.4	1.3	7:11	19:33	1:26	13:50	7:10	19:33	3:39	16:01	7:00	19:23	1:37	14:01	7:05	19:28	1:04	13:28
7	THUR	4.5	4.4	1.4	1.1	7:48	20:15	2:05	14:34	7:47	20:13	4:13	16:32	7:36	20:01	2:16	14:37	7:43	20:10	1:44	14:09
8	FRI	4.6	4.4	1.4	1.1	8:25	20:55	2:49	15:15	8:23	20:51	4:42	17:00	8:11	20:38	2:48	15:10	8:20	20:49	2:23	14:47
9	SAT	4.6	4.4	1.4	1.1	9:02	21:33	3:29	15:56	8:58	21:27	5:09	17:29	8:45	21:14	3:20	15:43	8:56	21:25	3:00	15:25
10	SUN	4.6	4.3	1.4	1.1	9:40	22:13	4:08	16:37	9:33	22:05	5:36	17:57	9:19	21:50	3:51	16:16	9:32	22:05	3:36	16:03
11	MON	4.6	4.3	1.5	1.1	10:17	22:52	4:45	17:18	10:09	22:42	6:03	18:25	9:54	22:26	4:24	16:49	10:09	22:43	4:12	16:42
12	TUES	4.5	4.2	1.6	1.1	10:56	23:33	5:25	17:59	10:45	23:20	6:30	18:53	10:29	23:03	4:56	17:22	10:46	23:22	4:49	17:19
13	WED	4.5		1.7	1.3	11:36	NT	6:06	18:44	11:23	NT	6:59	19:24	11:06	23:45	5:29	17:59	11:25	NT	5:27	18:02
14	THUR	4.3	4.2	1.8	1.4	0:19	12:24	6:52	19:36	0:03	12:08	7:31	19:58	11:50	NT	6:07	18:39	0:06	12:11	6:10	18:49
15	FRI	4.0	4.3	1.9	1.5	1:11	13:19	7:48	20:34	0:52	13:00	8:07	20:47	0:33	12:40	6:51	19:29	0:56	13:05	7:01	19:44
16	SAT	3.9	4.2	1.9	1.6	2:05	14:19	8:49	21:29	1:47	14:01	9:08	22:02	1:28	13:42	7:48	20:36	1:51	14:05	8:00	20:43
17	SUN	4.1	4.3	1.9	1.5	3:05	15:26	9:52	22:30	2:50	15:12	10:33	23:27	2:33	14:55	9:03	21:53	2:52	15:14	9:07	21:50
18	MON	4.1	4.3	1.7	1.4	4:10	16:35	10:56	23:28	3:59	16:25	NT	12:05	3:43	16:10	10:27	23:07	4:00	16:25	10:19	22:54
19	TUES	4.3	4.5	1.4		5:10	17:38	11:55	NT	5:02	17:32	0:49	13:27	4:48	17:19	11:42	NT	5:01	17:30	11:24	23:54
20	WED	4.5	4.7	1.0	1.2	6:05	18:35	0:22	12:48	6:00	18:32	2:06	14:44	5:48	18:21	0:17	12:51	5:57	18:28	NT	12:23
21	THUR	4.8	4.9	1.1	0.7	6:55	19:27	1:12	13:38	6:53	19:27	3:19	15:53	6:42	19:17	1:19	13:53	6:49	19:22	0:49	13:18
22	FRI	5.1	5.0	0.9	0.4	7:44	20:21	2:02	14:37	7:44	20:19	4:11	16:34	7:33	20:07	2:13	14:40	7:40	20:16	1:41	14:13
23	SAT	5.3	5.0	0.8	0.2	8:36	21:13	2:59	15:32	8:33	21:08	4:50	17:12	8:21	20:55	2:58	15:23	8:30	21:06	2:33	15:03
24	SUN	5.3	4.9	0.8	0.2	9:25	22:03	3:52	16:24	9:19	21:55	5:25	17:48	9:06	21:41	3:39	16:07	9:17	21:54	3:21	15:52
25	MON	5.2	4.8	0.8	0.3	10:14	22:51	4:42	17:16	10:06	22:41	6:01	18:24	9:51	22:25	4:21	16:47	10:06	22:42	4:09	16:39
26	TUES	5.0	4.6	1.0	0.6	11:02	23:41	5:32	18:07	10:51	23:28	6:34	18:59	10:35	23:11	4:59	17:30	10:52	23:30	4:54	17:28
27	WED	4.8		1.4	1.2	11:53	NT	6:23	19:00	11:39	NT	7:10	19:36	11:22	23:58	5:42	18:11	11:41	NT	5:42	18:16
28	THUR	4.3	4.5	1.5	1.3	0:33	12:47	7:17	19:58	0:17	12:30	7:45	20:13	NT	12:11	6:24	18:57	0:21	12:34	6:31	19:10
29	FRI	4.1	4.2	1.7	1.6	1:32	13:46	8:19	20:55	1:12	13:26	8:29	21:15	0:52	13:06	7:14	19:54	1:17	13:31	7:29	20:06
30	SAT	3.9	4.0	2.0	1.8	2:28	14:47	9:17	21:53	2:11	14:31	9:45	22:34	1:53	14:13	8:20	21:04	2:14	14:34	8:29	21:08
31	SUN	3.9	3.9	2.0	1.9	3:32	15:57	10:19	22:53	3:19	15:45	11:14	NT	3:02	15:29	9:42	22:24	3:21	15:46	9:39	22:16

JULY 2005

"NT" = No Tide

	BURNHAM OVERY STAITHE		WELLS BAR				WELLS QUAY				HEMSBY				Gt.YARMOUTH BRITANNIA PIER				
	HIGH WATER		HIGH WATER		LOW WATER		HIGH WATER		LOW WATER		HIGH WATER		LOW WATER		HIGH WATER		LOW WATER		
	AM	PM	AM	PM	AM	PM	AM	PM	AM	PM	AM	PM	AM	PM	AM	PM	AM	PM	
1	3:19	15:31	2:51	15:03	8:58	21:34	3:09	15:21	10:36	23:15	4:10	16:22	10:53	23:25	5:26	17:02	11:29	NT	--
2	4:12	16:36	3:52	16:06	10:01	22:32	4:12	16:26	11:45	NT	5:08	17:21	11:48	NT	6:20	18:06	0:07	12:30	--
3	5:17	17:35	4:46	17:04	10:59	23:25	5:07	17:25	0:18	12:47	5:59	18:16	0:17	12:40	7:07	19:07	0:59	13:26	--
4	6:08	18:28	5:36	17:55	11:51	NT	5:58	18:18	1:16	13:44	6:46	19:04	1:02	13:26	7:50	20:01	1:49	14:15	--
5	6:54	19:15	6:20	18:41	0:11	12:36	6:44	19:05	2:06	14:33	7:28	19:48	1:44	14:05	8:29	20:50	2:33	14:59	--
6	7:35	19:58	7:00	19:23	0:54	13:18	7:25	19:48	2:53	15:17	8:06	20:28	2:21	14:45	9:05	21:35	3:14	15:41	--
7	8:11	20:36	7:37	20:03	1:33	13:58	8:01	20:26	3:31	15:54	8:43	21:10	3:00	15:29	9:40	22:18	3:52	16:20	---
8	8:46	21:13	8:13	20:41	2:11	14:35	8:36	21:03	4:05	16:28	9:20	21:50	3:44	16:10	10:14	22:59	4:29	16:59	---
9	9:20	21:49	8:48	21:17	2:47	15:12	9:10	21:39	4:38	17:02	9:57	22:28	4:24	16:51	10:47	23:37	5:05	17:36	---
10	9:54	22:25	9:23	21:55	3:22	15:49	9:44	22:15	5:10	17:36	10:35	23:08	5:03	17:32	11:20	23:59	5:39	18:14	--
11	10:29	23:01	9:59	22:32	3:57	16:26	10:19	22:51	5:43	18:09	11:12	23:47	5:40	18:13	11:53	NT	6:14	18:53	--
12	11:04	23:38	10:35	23:10	4:33	17:03	10:54	23:28	6:16	18:44	11:51	NT	6:20	18:54	0:58	12:28	6:50	19:33	--
13	11:41	NT	11:13	23:53	5:10	17:44	11:31	NT	6:50	19:21	0:28	12:31	7:01	19:39	1:39	13:05	7:27	20:16	-
14	0:20	12:25	11:58	NT	5:52	18:30	0:10	12:15	7:29	20:03	1:14	13:19	7:47	20:31	2:26	13:51	8:12	21:07	--
15	1:08	13:15	0:42	12:50	6:42	19:24	0:58	13:05	8:15	20:54	2:06	14:14	8:43	21:29	3:19	14:46	9:06	22:03	--
16	2:03	14:17	1:37	13:51	7:41	20:25	1:53	14:07	9:13	22:00	3:00	15:14	9:44	22:24	4:16	15:52	10:09	23:04	--
17	3:08	15:30	2:40	15:02	8:50	21:34	2:58	15:20	10:27	23:15	4:00	16:21	10:47	23:25	5:16	17:10	11:22	NT	--
18	4:18	16:45	3:49	16:15	10:04	22:40	4:08	16:35	11:48	NT	5:05	17:30	11:51	NT	6:16	18:27	0:10	12:35	--
19	5:23	17:54	4:52	17:22	11:11	23:42	5:13	17:44	0:27	13:01	6:05	18:33	0:23	12:50	7:11	19:40	1:12	13:40	---
20	6:23	18:56	5:50	18:22	NT	12:12	6:13	18:46	1:35	14:08	7:00	19:30	1:17	13:43	8:05	20:43	2:11	14:40	---
21	7:17	19:52	6:43	19:17	0:38	13:08	7:07	19:42	2:35	15:08	7:50	20:22	2:07	14:33	8:56	21:41	3:05	15:35	-----
22	8:08	20:42	7:34	20:09	1:30	14:01	7:58	20:32	3:28	15:56	8:39	21:16	2:57	15:32	9:47	22:35	3:56	16:28	-----
23	8:56	21:30	8:23	20:58	2:21	14:50	8:46	21:20	4:15	16:41	9:31	22:08	3:54	16:27	10:35	23:25	4:46	17:18	-----
24	9:41	22:16	9:09	21:45	3:08	15:38	9:31	22:06	4:58	17:26	10:20	22:58	4:47	17:19	11:21	NT	5:33	18:07	-----
25	10:26	23:00	9:56	22:31	3:54	16:24	10:16	22:50	5:40	18:08	11:09	23:46	5:37	18:11	0:14	12:05	6:19	18:54	-----
26	11:10	23:46	10:41	23:18	4:38	17:11	11:00	23:36	6:20	18:51	11:57	NT	6:27	19:02	1:01	12:48	7:03	19:42	---
27	11:57	NT	11:29	NT	5:25	17:58	11:47	NT	7:04	19:34	0:36	12:48	7:18	19:55	1:49	13:32	7:49	20:32	--
28	0:33	12:46	0:07	12:20	6:13	18:50	0:23	12:36	7:48	20:21	1:28	13:42	8:12	20:53	2:39	14:22	8:40	21:28	---
29	1:27	13:41	1:02	13:16	7:09	19:47	1:17	13:31	8:39	21:19	2:27	14:41	9:14	21:50	3:36	15:20	9:39	22:27	--
30	2:28	14:48	2:01	14:21	8:11	20:51	2:18	14:38	9:45	22:28	3:23	15:42	10:12	22:48	4:36	16:30	10:46	23:31	-
31	3:37	16:04	3:09	15:35	9:23	22:01	3:27	15:54	11:04	23:45	4:27	16:52	11:14	23:48	5:39	17:46	11:59	NT	

AUGUST 2005

"NT" = No Tide

		Heights at CROMER				CROMER SHERINGHAM				KING'S LYNN QUAY				HUNSTANTON				BLAKENEY BAR			
		HIGH		LOW		HIGH WATER		LOW WATER		HIGH WATER		LOW WATER		HIGH WATER		LOW WATER		HIGH WATER		LOW WATER	
		AM	PM	AM	PM	AM	PM	AM	PM	AM	PM	AM	PM	AM	PM	AM	PM	AM	PM	AM	PM
1	MON	3.9	3.9	2.0	1.9	4:37	17:02	11:22	23:48	4:27	16:54	0:01	12:42	4:12	16:40	11:01	23:31	4:27	16:53	10:48	23:1
2	TUES	4.0	4.0		1.7	5:31	17:57	NT	12:15	5:24	17:52	1:16	13:55	5:11	17:40	NT	12:06	5:22	17:49	11:46	NT
3	WED	4.1	4.1	1.8	1.5	6:17	18:43	0:34	12:57	6:13	18:41	2:24	15:01	6:01	18:30	0:33	13:04	6:10	18:37	0:08	12:3
4	THUR	4.3	4.3	1.6	1.3	6:57	19:23	1:13	13:36	6:55	19:23	3:23	15:51	6:44	19:13	1:24	13:51	6:51	19:18	0:52	13:1
5	FRI	4.5	4.5	1.4	1.1	7:32	20:00	1:52	14:18	7:32	19:59	4:03	16:21	7:22	19:48	2:03	14:25	7:27	19:55	1:30	13:5
6	SAT	4.7	4.5	1.4	0.9	8:07	20:36	2:31	14:56	8:06	20:33	4:30	16:47	7:55	20:21	2:34	14:55	8:02	20:30	2:06	14:30
7	SUN	4.7	4.5	1.3	0.8	8:42	21:11	3:07	15:34	8:39	21:06	4:56	17:13	8:27	20:53	3:06	15:25	8:36	21:04	2:41	15:0
8	MON	4.8	4.5	1.2	0.8	9:16	21:46	3:43	16:11	9:11	21:39	5:20	17:38	8:58	21:25	3:34	15:54	9:09	21:38	3:14	15:3
9	TUES	4.8	4.5	1.2	0.8	9:50	22:19	4:18	16:45	9:43	22:10	5:44	18:03	9:29	21:55	4:01	16:24	9:42	22:10	3:46	16:1
10	WED	4.7	4.4	1.3	0.9	10:24	22:55	4:54	17:22	10:15	22:44	6:08	18:28	10:00	22:28	4:29	16:53	10:15	22:45	4:19	16:4
11	THUR	4.7	4.3	1.4	1.1	11:02	23:34	5:31	18:02	10:51	23:21	6:33	18:56	10:35	23:04	4:58	17:25	10:52	23:23	4:53	17:2
12	FRI	4.5		1.5	1.3	11:43	NT	6:10	18:47	11:30	NT	7:02	19:27	11:13	23:45	5:33	18:02	11:32	NT	5:31	18:0
13	SAT	4.3	4.1	1.7	1.5	0:19	12:34	7:01	19:43	0:03	12:18	7:34	20:03	11:59	NT	6:12	18:46	0:06	12:22	6:17	18:5
14	SUN	4.0	4.1	1.8	1.7	1:15	13:41	8:05	20:49	0:56	13:21	8:19	21:08	0:36	13:01	7:04	19:48	1:01	13:26	7:17	20:00
15	MON	3.9	4.1	1.8	1.8	2:21	14:57	9:18	22:00	2:04	14:42	9:46	22:45	1:45	14:24	8:21	21:15	2:08	14:45	8:30	21:17
16	TUES	4.0	4.1	1.7	1.7	3:38	16:20	10:34	23:12	3:25	16:10	11:35	NT	3:09	15:55	10:01	22:47	3:26	16:10	9:56	22:37
17	WED	4.0	4.3	1.4		4:51	17:31	11:45	NT	4:42	17:24	0:27	13:13	4:28	17:11	11:28	NT	4:41	17:22	11:13	23:4
18	THUR	4.5	4.6	1.4	0.9	5:51	18:29	0:12	12:41	5:46	18:26	1:51	14:32	5:33	18:15	0:03	12:40	5:44	18:22	NT	12:14
19	FRI	4.9	4.9	1.1	0.5	6:43	19:18	1:02	13:30	6:41	19:18	3:07	15:43	6:30	19:08	1:09	13:41	6:37	19:13	0:39	13:08
20	SAT	5.2	5.1	0.8	0.2	7:30	20:05	1:51	14:21	7:30	20:04	4:02	16:24	7:20	19:53	2:02	14:28	7:25	20:00	1:29	13:58
21	SUN	5.4	5.1	0.6	0.1	8:17	20:52	2:40	15:12	8:15	20:48	4:37	16:58	8:03	20:35	2:43	15:07	8:12	20:46	2:16	14:4
22	MON	5.5	5.1	0.5	0.1	9:03	21:37	3:30	16:00	8:59	21:31	5:10	17:32	8:46	21:17	3:21	15:47	8:57	21:30	3:01	15:30
23	TUES	5.3	4.9	0.6	0.2	9:49	22:21	4:16	16:46	9:42	22:12	5:42	18:04	9:28	21:57	3:59	16:25	9:41	22:12	3:44	16:13
24	WED	5.1	4.7	0.8	0.5	10:33	23:04	5:01	17:33	10:24	22:53	6:14	18:28	10:09	22:37	4:36	17:00	10:24	22:54	4:26	16:55
25	THUR	4.8	4.4	1.1	1.0	11:18	23:50	5:46	18:18	11:06	23:36	6:45	19:06	10:50	23:19	5:13	17:37	11:07	23:38	5:08	17:37
26	FRI		4.1	1.4	1.4	NT	12:06	6:35	19:04	11:51	NT	7:17	19:38	11:33	NT	5:50	18:17	11:54	NT	5:52	18:22
27	SAT	4.5	4.1	1.7	1.8	0:37	13:00	7:26	20:05	0:21	12:42	7:52	20:19	0:02	12:23	6:33	19:04	0:25	12:46	6:41	19:17
28	SUN	3.9	3.8	2.0	2.1	1:39	14:07	8:34	21:09	1:19	13:49	8:47	21:35	0:59	13:30	7:29	20:12	1:24	13:53	7:44	20:21
29	MON	3.7	3.7	2.2	2.3	2:45	15:29	9:46	22:25	2:29	15:16	10:26	23:21	2:11	14:59	8:57	21:48	2:32	15:18	9:01	21:45
30	TUES	3.7	3.7	2.1	2.1	4:05	16:50	11:03	23:34	3:54	16:41	NT	12:13	3:38	16:27	10:34	23:13	3:55	16:40	10:26	23:00
31	WED	3.8	3.9		2.0	5:12	17:47	NT	12:02	5:04	17:42	0:56	13:36	4:50	17:29	11:49	NT	5:03	17:40	11:31	23:53

AUGUST 2005

"NT" = No Tide

BURNHAM Overy Staithe		WELLS BAR				WELLS QUAY				HEMSBY				Gt.YARMOUTH BRITANNIA PIER			
HIGH WATER		HIGH WATER		LOW WATER		HIGH WATER		LOW WATER		HIGH WATER		LOW WATER		HIGH WATER		LOW WATER	
AM	PM	AM	PM	AM	PM	AM	PM	AM	PM	AM	PM	AM	PM	AM	PM	AM	PM
4:47	17:15	4:17	16:44	10:34	23:02	4:37	17:05	NT	12:21	5:32	17:57	NT	12:17	6:35	18:53	0:35	13:04
5:46	18:15	5:14	17:42	11:33	23:56	5:36	18:05	0:50	13:24	6:26	18:52	0:43	13:10	7:22	19:52	1:28	13:58
6:36	19:05	6:03	18:31	NT	12:23	6:26	18:55	1:50	14:20	7:12	19:38	1:29	13:52	8:05	20:43	2:16	14:45
7:19	19:48	6:45	19:13	0:41	13:06	7:09	19:38	2:39	15:06	7:52	20:18	2:08	14:31	8:44	21:26	2:59	15:26
7:57	20:23	7:22	19:49	1:20	13:44	7:47	20:13	3:19	15:41	8:27	20:55	2:47	15:13	9:20	22:04	3:37	16:04
8:30	20:56	7:56	20:23	1:55	14:18	8:20	20:46	3:51	16:12	9:02	21:31	3:26	15:51	9:54	22:40	4:12	16:39
9:02	**21:28**	**8:29**	**20:56**	**2:29**	**14:52**	**8:52**	**21:18**	**4:23**	**16:43**	**9:37**	**22:06**	**4:02**	**16:29**	**10:27**	**23:15**	**4:45**	**17:14**
9:33	22:00	9:01	21:29	3:01	15:25	9:23	21:50	4:52	17:13	10:11	22:41	4:38	17:06	10:59	23:48	5:17	17:48
10:04	22:30	9:33	22:00	3:32	15:57	9:54	22:20	5:20	17:43	10:45	23:14	5:13	17:40	11:30	NT	5:49	18:21
10:35	23:03	10:05	22:34	4:04	16:30	10:25	22:53	5:49	18:17	11:19	23:50	5:49	18:17	0:21	12:03	6:20	18:57
11:10	23:39	10:41	23:11	4:37	17:06	11:00	23:29	6:19	18:47	11:57	NT	6:26	18:57	0:57	12:38	6:54	19:36
11:48	NT	11:20	23:53	5:14	17:47	11:38	NT	6:54	19:24	0:29	12:38	7:05	19:42	1:36	13:20	7:33	20:21
0:20	12:34	NT	12:08	5:59	18:37	0:10	12:24	7:35	20:10	1:14	13:29	7:56	20:38	2:21	14:14	8:23	21:17
1:11	**13:36**	**0:46**	**13:11**	**6:57**	**19:41**	**1:01**	**13:26**	**8:28**	**21:13**	**2:10**	**14:36**	**9:00**	**21:44**	**3:18**	**15:26**	**9:29**	**22:22**
2:20	14:59	1:54	14:32	8:12	21:00	2:10	14:49	9:46	22:38	3:16	15:52	10:13	22:55	4:27	16:55	10:52	23:43
3:44	16:30	3:15	16:00	9:40	22:22	3:34	16:20	11:22	NT	4:33	17:15	11:29	NT	5:39	18:23	NT	12:17
5:03	17:46	4:32	17:14	10:59	23:30	4:53	17:36	0:07	12:47	5:46	18:26	0:07	12:40	6:45	19:37	0:56	13:29
6:08	18:50	5:36	18:16	NT	12:03	5:58	18:40	1:21	13:58	6:46	19:24	1:07	13:36	7:45	20:39	1:58	14:30
7:05	19:43	6:31	19:08	0:28	12:58	6:55	19:33	2:25	14:57	7:38	20:13	1:57	14:25	8:40	21:32	2:53	15:24
7:55	20:28	7:20	19:54	1:19	13:47	7:45	20:18	3:18	15:44	8:25	21:00	2:46	15:16	9:31	22:19	3:43	16:13
8:38	**21:10**	**8:05**	**20:38**	**2:04**	**14:32**	**8:28**	**21:00**	**3:59**	**16:25**	**9:12**	**21:47**	**3:35**	**16:07**	**10:18**	**23:04**	**4:29**	**16:59**
9:21	21:52	8:49	21:21	2:48	15:16	9:11	21:42	4:39	17:05	9:58	22:32	4:25	16:55	11:02	23:47	5:12	17:43
10:03	22:32	9:32	22:02	3:30	15:58	9:53	22:22	5:18	17:44	10:44	23:16	5:11	17:41	11:44	NT	5:54	18:26
10:44	23:12	10:14	22:43	4:11	16:39	10:34	23:02	5:56	18:21	11:28	23:59	5:56	18:28	0:28	12:23	6:35	19:08
11:25	23:54	10:56	23:26	4:52	17:20	11:15	23:44	6:34	18:59	NT	12:13	6:41	19:13	1:07	13:04	7:15	19:52
NT	12:08	11:41	NT	5:35	18:04	11:58	NT	7:13	19:40	0:45	13:01	7:30	20:01	1:50	13:49	8:00	20:40
0:37	12:58	0:11	12:32	6:22	18:57	0:27	12:48	7:56	20:28	1:32	13:55	8:21	21:00	2:36	14:47	8:53	21:41
1:34	**14:05**	**1:09**	**13:39**	**7:24**	**20:03**	**1:24**	**13:55**	**8:54**	**21:37**	**2:34**	**15:02**	**9:29**	**22:04**	**3:38**	**16:05**	**10:06**	**22:52**
2:46	15:34	2:19	15:06	8:44	21:29	2:36	15:24	10:21	23:10	3:40	16:24	10:41	23:20	4:48	17:34	11:29	NT
4:13	17:02	3:44	16:31	10:11	22:46	4:03	16:52	11:55	NT	5:00	17:45	11:58	NT	5:57	18:50	0:09	12:44
5:25	18:04	4:54	17:32	11:18	23:41	5:15	17:54	0:33	13:08	6:07	18:42	0:29	12:57	6:52	19:45	1:12	13:40

SEPTEMBER 2005

"NT" = No Tide

		CROMER HIGH AM	CROMER HIGH PM	CROMER LOW AM	CROMER LOW PM	CROMER SHERINGHAM HIGH WATER AM	PM	LOW WATER AM	PM	KING'S LYNN QUAY HIGH WATER AM	PM	LOW WATER AM	PM	HUNSTANTON HIGH WATER AM	PM	LOW WATER AM	PM	BLAKENEY BAR HIGH WATER AM	PM	LOW WATER AM	PM
1	THUR	4.1	4.1	1.5	1.2	5:59	18:30	0:21	12:44	5:54	18:27	2:05	14:21	5:42	18:16	0:16	12:43	5:51	18:23	NT	12:1
2	FRI	4.3	4.3	1.7	1.2	6:37	19:05	0:58	13:18	6:34	19:04	2:47	15:14	6:23	18:54	1:05	13:29	6:30	18:59	0:35	12:5
3	SAT	4.5	4.5	1.4	1.0	7:10	19:37	1:32	13:53	7:09	19:37	3:30	15:49	6:59	19:27	1:43	14:04	7:04	19:32	1:10	13:3
4	SUN	4.7	4.7	1.3	0.8	7:41	20:08	2:04	14:29	7:41	20:07	3:57	16:13	7:30	19:56	2:15	14:32	7:37	20:03	1:43	14:0
5	MON	4.9	4.7	1.1	0.7	8:14	20:41	2:39	15:02	8:12	20:38	4:21	16:37	8:00	20:26	2:42	15:01	8:09	20:35	2:15	14:3
6	TUES	5.0	4.7	1.0	0.6	8:47	21:12	3:14	15:37	8:43	21:07	4:45	17:01	8:31	20:54	3:09	15:28	8:40	21:05	2:46	15:0
7	WED	5.0	4.7	1.0	0.7	9:18	21:45	3:45	16:12	9:13	21:38	5:07	17:24	9:00	21:24	3:36	15:55	9:11	21:37	3:16	15:4
8	THUR	4.9	4.6	1.0	0.8	9:53	22:19	4:21	16:46	9:46	22:10	5:31	17:49	9:32	21:55	4:04	16:25	9:45	22:10	3:49	16:1
9	FRI	4.8	4.5	1.1	1.0	10:30	22:56	4:58	17:25	10:21	22:45	5:56	18:15	10:06	22:29	4:33	16:56	10:21	22:46	4:23	16:4
10	SAT	4.5	4.3	1.3	1.3	11:13	23:39	5:39	18:08	11:01	23:26	6:25	18:45	10:45	23:09	5:06	17:31	11:02	23:28	5:01	17:2
11	SUN		4.1	1.5	1.7	NT	12:06	6:28	19:06	11:51	NT	6:59	19:23	11:33	NT	5:47	18:17	11:54	NT	5:47	18:2
12	MON	4.1	4.1	1.7	1.9	0:39	13:20	7:38	20:24	0:22	13:01	7:45	20:19	0:03	12:41	6:41	19:19	0:26	13:06	6:51	19:3
13	TUES	3.9	3.9	1.8	2.0	1:56	14:50	9:05	21:47	1:37	14:34	9:12	22:12	1:18	14:16	8:04	20:58	1:41	14:37	8:16	21:0
14	WED	3.9	4.1	1.7	1.9	3:22	16:19	10:29	23:05	3:08	16:08	11:11	NT	2:51	15:53	9:52	22:36	3:10	16:08	9:49	22:2
15	THUR	4.2	4.3	1.3		4:39	17:27	11:37	NT	4:30	17:20	0:01	12:48	4:15	17:07	11:20	23:52	4:30	17:18	11:05	23:3
16	FRI	4.6	4.7	0.8	1.1	5:39	18:20	0:05	12:30	5:33	18:16	1:25	14:04	5:20	18:04	NT	12:29	5:31	18:13	NT	12:0
17	SAT	4.9	4.9	0.8	0.4	6:29	19:03	0:52	13:15	6:26	19:02	2:34	15:10	6:15	18:52	0:55	13:26	6:22	18:57	0:27	12:5
18	SUN	5.3	5.1	0.8	0.2	7:12	19:44	1:31	14:00	7:11	19:44	3:31	15:54	7:01	19:33	1:46	14:11	7:06	19:40	1:11	13:3
19	MON	5.4	5.2	0.5	0.0	7:56	20:27	2:19	14:47	7:55	20:24	4:07	16:25	7:44	20:12	2:26	14:46	7:51	20:21	1:56	14:2
20	TUES	5.4	5.1	0.5	0.1	8:38	21:06	3:03	15:31	8:35	21:02	4:38	16:56	8:23	20:49	3:02	15:22	8:32	21:00	2:37	15:0
21	WED	5.3	5.0	0.5	0.4	9:20	21:46	3:48	16:13	9:15	21:39	5:07	17:25	9:02	21:25	3:35	15:56	9:13	21:38	3:17	15:4
22	THUR	5.1	4.7	0.7	0.7	10:02	22:26	4:27	16:54	9:54	22:17	5:36	17:53	9:40	22:02	4:10	16:29	9:53	22:17	3:55	16:1
23	FRI	4.7	4.4	1.0	1.1	10:43	23:05	5:09	17:35	10:33	22:54	6:05	18:21	10:18	22:38	4:44	17:02	10:33	22:55	4:34	16:5
24	SAT	4.3	4.1	1.4	1.6	11:27	23:49	5:55	18:19	11:15	23:35	6:34	18:52	10:58	23:18	5:18	17:38	11:17	23:37	5:13	17:3
25	SUN		3.8	1.7	2.0	NT	12:20	6:42	19:11	NT	12:04	7:08	19:27	11:46	NT	5:57	18:22	NT	12:07	6:00	18:2
26	MON	3.9	3.7	2.0	2.3	0:44	13:34	7:48	20:29	0:27	13:14	7:52	20:26	0:08	12:54	6:51	19:24	0:31	13:19	7:01	19:3
27	TUES	3.6	3.6	2.2	2.4	2:01	15:07	9:16	21:57	1:42	14:52	9:29	22:27	1:23	14:35	8:19	21:12	1:46	14:54	8:28	21:1
28	WED	3.6	3.7	2.1	2.3	3:30	16:32	10:38	23:10	3:17	16:22	11:25	NT	3:00	16:07	10:05	22:45	3:19	16:22	10:00	22:3
29	THUR	3.8	3.9	1.8	2.0	4:41	17:27	11:38	23:59	4:32	17:20	0:09	12:46	4:17	17:07	11:17	23:46	4:32	17:18	11:04	23:2
30	FRI	4.1	4.1		1.7	5:30	18:05	NT	12:19	5:23	18:00	1:17	13:45	5:10	17:48	NT	12:10	5:21	17:57	11:49	NT

Times BST

SEPTEMBER 2005

"NT" = No Tide

	BURNHAM OVERY STAITHE		WELLS BAR				WELLS QUAY				HEMSBY				Gt.YARMOUTH BRITANNIA PIER				
	HIGH WATER		HIGH WATER		LOW WATER		HIGH WATER		LOW WATER		HIGH WATER		LOW WATER		HIGH WATER		LOW WATER		
	AM	PM	AM	PM	AM	PM	AM	PM	AM	PM	AM	PM	AM	PM	AM	PM	AM	PM	
	6:17	18:51	5:44	18:17	NT	12:06	6:07	18:41	1:16	14:01	6:54	19:25	1:16	13:39	7:37	20:29	1:59	14:25	--
	6:58	19:29	6:24	18:54	0:24	12:46	6:48	19:19	2:21	14:45	7:32	20:00	1:53	14:13	8:18	21:07	2:40	15:04	--
	7:34	20:02	6:59	19:27	1:00	13:21	7:24	19:52	2:59	15:20	8:05	20:32	2:27	14:48	8:54	21:41	3:15	15:39	---
	8:05	**20:31**	**7:31**	**19:57**	**1:32**	**13:53**	**7:55**	**20:21**	**3:30**	**15:49**	**8:36**	**21:03**	**2:59**	**15:24**	**9:29**	**22:13**	**3:48**	**16:12**	----
	8:35	21:01	8:02	20:28	2:03	14:24	8:25	20:51	3:58	16:18	9:09	21:36	3:34	15:57	10:02	22:45	4:19	16:45	----
	9:06	21:29	8:33	20:57	2:34	14:55	8:56	21:19	4:27	16:46	9:42	22:07	4:09	16:32	10:34	23:15	4:51	17:16	----
	9:35	21:59	9:03	21:28	3:03	15:26	9:25	21:49	4:54	17:14	10:13	22:40	4:40	17:07	11:06	23:46	5:20	17:49	----
	10:07	22:30	9:36	22:00	3:35	15:58	9:57	22:20	5:23	17:44	10:48	23:14	5:16	17:41	11:40	NT	5:53	18:23	----
	10:41	23:04	10:11	22:35	4:08	16:33	10:31	22:54	5:53	18:16	11:25	23:51	5:53	18:20	0:18	12:16	6:27	19:01	---
	11:20	23:44	10:51	23:16	4:45	17:12	11:10	23:34	6:27	18:52	NT	12:08	6:34	19:03	0:53	13:00	7:06	19:45	---
	NT	**12:08**	**11:41**	**NT**	**5:30**	**18:04**	**11:58**	**NT**	**7:09**	**19:40**	**0:34**	**13:01**	**7:23**	**20:01**	**1:35**	**13:59**	**7:58**	**20:45**	-
	0:38	13:16	0:12	12:51	6:32	19:14	0:28	13:06	8:05	20:44	1:34	14:15	8:33	21:19	2:34	15:24	9:12	22:03	-
	1:53	14:51	1:27	14:24	7:57	20:45	1:43	14:41	9:29	22:22	2:51	15:45	10:00	22:42	3:49	17:03	10:44	23:30	-
	3:26	16:28	2:58	15:58	9:33	22:13	3:16	16:18	11:14	23:57	4:17	17:14	11:24	0:00	5:10	18:29	NT	12:10	--
	4:50	17:42	4:20	17:10	10:51	23:21	4:40	17:32	NT	12:39	5:34	18:22	NT	12:32	6:23	19:34	0:46	13:19	--
	5:55	18:49	5:23	18:06	11:52	NT	5:45	18:29	1:11	13:46	6:34	19:15	1:00	13:25	7:27	20:29	1:46	14:17	----
	6:50	19:27	6:16	18:52	0:16	12:43	6:40	19:17	2:12	14:41	7:24	19:58	1:47	14:10	8:23	21:15	2:39	15:07	-----
	7:36	**20:08**	**7:01**	**19:34**	**1:01**	**13:28**	**7:26**	**19:58**	**3:01**	**15:26**	**8:07**	**20:39**	**2:26**	**14:55**	**9:12**	**21:58**	**3:25**	**15:52**	------
	8:19	20:47	7:45	20:14	1:45	14:09	8:09	20:37	3:42	16:03	8:51	21:22	3:14	15:42	9:58	22:37	4:08	16:34	------
	8:58	21:24	8:25	20:52	2:25	14:49	8:48	21:14	4:19	16:40	9:33	22:01	3:58	16:26	10:39	23:15	4:48	17:15	-----
	9:37	22:00	9:05	21:29	3:04	15:27	9:27	21:50	4:54	17:15	10:15	22:41	4:43	17:08	11:18	23:50	5:27	17:53	-----
	10:15	22:37	9:44	22:07	3:41	16:04	10:05	22:27	5:29	17:49	10:57	23:21	5:22	17:49	11:56	NT	6:04	18:32	----
	10:53	23:13	10:23	22:44	4:19	16:41	10:43	23:03	6:04	18:23	11:38	0:00	6:04	18:30	0:25	12:35	6:43	19:10	---
	11:33	23:53	11:05	23:25	4:57	17:21	11:23	23:43	6:39	19:00	NT	12:22	6:46	19:14	0:58	13:20	7:24	19:54	--
	NT	**12:21**	**11:54**	**NT**	**5:42**	**18:09**	**NT**	**12:11**	**7:19**	**19:45**	**0:44**	**13:15**	**7:37**	**20:06**	**1:39**	**14:22**	**8:17**	**20:52**	--
	0:43	13:29	0:17	13:04	6:42	19:19	0:33	13:19	8:15	20:49	1:39	14:29	8:43	21:24	2:34	15:52	9:31	22:14	
	1:58	15:10	1:32	14:42	8:10	20:57	1:48	15:00	9:44	22:35	2:56	16:02	10:11	22:52	3:51	17:28	11:01	23:42	
	3:35	16:42	3:07	16:12	9:44	22:20	3:25	16:32	11:26	NT	4:25	17:27	11:33	NT	5:09	18:37	NT	12:16	
	4:52	17:42	4:22	17:10	10:50	23:15	4:42	17:32	0:05	12:37	5:36	18:22	0:05	12:33	6:10	19:26	0:46	13:10	
	5:45	18:23	5:13	17:50	11:37	23:54	5:35	18:13	1:05	13:29	6:25	19:00	0:54	13:14	6:59	20:04	1:33	13:54	--

OCTOBER 2005

"NT" = No Tide

		Heights at CROMER				CROMER SHERINGHAM				KING'S LYNN QUAY				HUNSTANTON				BLAKENEY BAR			
Times BST/ GMT		HIGH		LOW		HIGH WATER		LOW WATER		HIGH WATER		LOW WATER		HIGH WATER		LOW WATER		HIGH WATER		LOW WATER	
		AM	PM	AM	PM	AM	PM	AM	PM	AM	PM	AM	PM	AM	PM	AM	PM	AM	PM	AM	PM
1	SAT	4.3	4.4	1.1	0.8	6:07	18:38	0:32	12:51	6:02	18:35	2:06	14:32	5:50	18:24	0:31	12:54	5:59	18:31	0:06	12:2
2	SUN	4.6	4.6	1.4	0.9	6:41	19:07	1:05	13:21	6:38	19:06	2:55	15:18	6:27	18:56	1:12	13:32	6:34	19:01	0:42	12:5
3	MON	4.8	4.7	1.2	0.7	7:10	19:36	1:32	13:53	7:09	19:36	3:32	15:49	6:59	19:26	1:47	14:04	7:04	19:31	1:12	13:3
4	TUES	4.9	4.9	1.0	0.6	7:42	20:07	2:05	14:29	7:42	20:06	3:58	16:13	7:31	19:55	2:16	14:32	7:38	20:02	1:44	14:0
5	WED	5.1	4.9	0.9	0.5	8:15	20:39	2:40	15:02	8:13	20:36	4:22	16:37	8:01	20:24	2:43	15:01	8:10	20:33	2:16	14:3
6	THUR	5.1	4.8	0.8	0.6	8:50	21:12	3:15	15:39	8:46	21:07	4:45	17:01	8:33	20:54	3:10	15:29	8:44	21:05	2:47	15:0
7	FRI	4.9	4.7	0.8	0.8	9:27	21:48	3:52	16:16	9:21	21:41	5:10	17:27	9:08	21:27	3:39	15:59	9:19	21:40	3:21	15:4
8	SAT	4.7	4.5	1.0	1.1	10:08	22:29	4:33	16:57	10:00	22:20	5:39	17:56	9:46	22:05	4:12	16:32	9:59	22:20	3:59	16:2
9	SUN	4.5	4.3	1.1	1.4	10:56	23:17	5:18	17:45	10:45	23:05	6:10	18:29	10:29	22:49	4:49	17:12	10:46	23:06	4:42	17:0
10	MON	4.2		1.4	1.7	11:55	NT	6:15	18:46	11:41	NT	6:49	19:11	11:24	23:46	5:34	18:01	11:43	NT	5:34	18:0
11	TUES	4.1	3.9	1.6	2.0	0:20	13:17	7:29	20:10	0:04	12:58	7:39	20:07	NT	12:38	6:36	19:09	0:07	13:03	6:44	19:2
12	WED	4.0	3.9	1.7	2.1	1:42	14:50	9:02	21:38	1:22	14:34	9:09	22:01	1:02	14:16	8:01	20:49	1:27	14:37	8:13	20:5
13	THUR	4.0	4.1	1.5	1.9	3:09	16:13	10:21	22:53	2:54	16:02	11:01	23:46	2:37	15:47	9:44	22:24	2:56	16:02	9:41	22:1
14	FRI	4.3	4.4	1.1	1.5	4:23	17:14	11:25	23:51	4:13	17:06	NT	12:30	3:58	16:52	11:04	23:34	4:13	17:05	10:51	23:1
15	SAT	4.6	4.7		1.1	5:21	18:01	NT	12:15	5:14	17:56	1:05	13:40	5:00	17:44	NT	12:06	5:13	17:53	11:46	NT
16	SUN	4.9	4.9	0.8	0.5	6:08	18:41	0:32	12:56	6:03	18:39	2:06	14:42	5:51	18:28	0:31	12:59	6:00	18:35	0:06	12:3
17	MON	5.1	5.1	0.6	0.3	6:51	19:19	1:13	13:33	6:49	19:19	3:05	15:33	6:38	19:09	1:20	13:48	6:45	19:14	0:50	13:1
18	TUES	5.3	5.1	0.6	0.2	7:31	19:58	1:53	14:17	7:31	19:57	3:49	16:06	7:21	19:46	2:04	14:24	7:26	19:53	1:31	13:5
19	WED	5.3	5.1	0.5	0.4	8:12	20:36	2:35	14:58	8:10	20:33	4:18	16:34	7:59	20:21	2:38	14:57	8:06	20:30	2:10	14:3
20	THUR	5.1	4.9	0.6	0.6	8:52	21:13	3:17	15:39	8:48	21:08	4:47	17:02	8:35	20:55	3:12	15:30	8:46	21:06	2:49	15:1
21	FRI	4.9	4.7	0.8	0.9	9:33	21:52	3:57	16:19	9:27	21:45	5:14	17:30	9:14	21:31	3:44	16:02	9:25	21:44	3:27	15:4
22	SAT	4.6	4.5	1.0	1.3	10:14	22:29	4:39	16:58	10:06	22:20	5:43	17:56	9:51	22:05	4:18	16:33	10:06	22:20	4:06	16:2
23	SUN	4.3	4.1	1.3	1.7	10:57	23:10	5:21	17:40	10:46	22:59	6:12	18:25	10:34	22:43	4:52	17:07	10:47	23:00	4:45	17:0
24	MON	3.9		1.6		11:50	NT	6:09	18:32	11:36	23:49	6:46	19:00	11:19	23:31	5:32	17:47	11:38	23:52	5:30	17:4
25	TUES	3.9	3.7	1.9	2.3	0:03	13:00	7:13	19:41	NT	12:42	7:29	19:47	NT	12:23	6:24	18:44	NT	12:46	6:29	18:5
26	WED	3.7	3.5	2.0	2.5	1:11	14:26	8:36	21:08	0:52	14:09	8:34	21:19	0:33	13:50	7:31	20:11	0:56	14:13	7:46	20:2
27	THUR	3.7	3.7	2.0	2.4	2:35	15:49	9:54	22:26	2:19	15:37	10:23	23:07	2:01	15:21	9:09	21:49	2:22	15:38	9:11	21:4
28	FRI	3.8	3.9	1.7	2.1	3:51	16:45	11:48	NT	3:39	16:36	11:48	NT	3:23	16:22	10:26	22:53	3:40	16:35	10:18	22:4
29	SAT	4.0	4.1	1.5	1.9	4:43	17:27	11:38	23:57	4:34	17:20	0:19	12:49	4:19	17:07	11:21	23:44	4:34	17:18	11:06	23:26
30	SUN	4.3	4.3	1.2	1.5	4:29	17:05	11:22	23:38	4:19	16:57	1:15	12:27	4:04	16:43	11:01	23:21	4:19	16:56	10:48	23:06
31	MON	4.5	4.5	1.0		5:07	17:36	11:56	NT	4:59	17:30	23:50	13:14	4:45	17:17	11:43	23:58	4:58	17:28	11:25	23:4

OCTOBER 2005

"NT" = No Tide

BURNHAM OVERY STAITHE		WELLS BAR				WELLS QUAY				HEMSBY				Gt.YARMOUTH BRITANNIA PIER				
HIGH WATER		HIGH WATER		LOW WATER		HIGH WATER		LOW WATER		HIGH WATER		LOW WATER		HIGH WATER		LOW WATER		
AM	PM	AM	PM	AM	PM	AM	PM	AM	PM	AM	PM	AM	PM	AM	PM	AM	PM	
6:25	18:59	5:52	18:25	NT	12:15	6:15	18:49	1:48	14:11	7:02	19:33	1:27	13:46	7:42	20:39	2:10	14:32	---
7:02	**19:31**	**6:28**	**18:56**	**0:31**	**12:49**	**6:52**	**19:21**	**2:28**	**14:48**	**7:36**	**20:02**	**2:00**	**14:16**	**8:22**	**21:11**	**2:46**	**15:07**	----
7:34	20:01	6:59	19:26	1:02	13:21	7:24	19:51	3:02	15:20	8:05	20:31	2:27	14:48	8:59	21:43	3:18	15:40	----
8:06	20:30	7:32	19:56	1:33	13:53	7:56	20:20	3:31	15:49	8:37	21:02	3:00	15:24	9:34	22:13	3:51	16:13	-----
8:36	20:59	8:03	20:26	2:04	14:24	8:26	20:49	3:59	16:18	9:10	21:34	3:35	15:57	10:09	22:43	4:22	16:45	----
9:08	21:29	8:36	20:57	2:35	14:56	8:58	21:19	4:28	16:47	9:45	22:07	4:10	16:33	10:44	23:14	4:55	17:19	-----
9:43	22:02	9:11	21:31	3:08	15:30	9:33	21:52	4:58	17:18	10:22	22:43	4:47	17:11	11:21	23:46	5:29	17:55	----
10:21	22:40	9:50	22:10	3:45	16:07	10:11	22:30	5:32	17:52	11:03	23:24	5:28	17:52	NT	12:03	6:07	18:35	---
11:04	**23:24**	**10:35**	**22:55**	**4:26**	**16:51**	**10:54**	**23:14**	**6:09**	**18:33**	**11:51**	**NT**	**6:13**	**18:40**	**0:22**	**12:54**	**6:53**	**19:22**	---
11:59	NT	11:31	23:54	5:17	17:46	11:49	NT	6:56	19:23	0:12	12:50	7:10	19:41	1:05	14:04	7:52	20:25	--
0:21	13:13	NT	12:48	6:25	19:02	0:11	13:03	7:59	20:33	1:15	14:12	8:24	21:05	2:04	15:37	9:11	21:49	-
1:37	14:51	1:12	14:24	7:54	20:36	1:27	14:41	9:26	22:13	2:37	15:45	9:57	22:33	3:20	17:11	10:39	23:17	
3:12	16:22	2:44	15:52	9:25	22:01	3:02	16:12	11:06	23:45	4:04	17:08	11:16	23:48	4:43	18:25	11:59	NT	-
4:33	17:27	4:03	16:56	10:37	23:05	4:23	17:17	NT	12:24	5:18	18:09	NT	12:20	5:59	19:22	0:31	13:03	---
5:35	18:19	5:04	17:46	11:33	23:54	5:25	18:09	0:54	13:24	6:16	18:56	0:46	13:10	7:04	20:08	1:29	13:56	----
6:26	**19:03**	**5:53**	**18:29**	**NT**	**12:20**	**6:16**	**18:53**	**1:48**	**14:16**	**7:03**	**19:36**	**1:27**	**13:51**	**8:00**	**20:51**	**2:17**	**14:43**	-----
7:13	19:44	6:39	19:09	0:39	13:03	7:03	19:34	2:36	15:03	7:46	20:14	2:08	14:28	8:49	21:31	3:02	15:27	------
7:56	20:21	7:21	19:47	1:21	13:43	7:46	20:11	3:20	15:40	8:26	20:53	2:48	15:12	9:33	22:08	3:44	16:07	-----
8:34	20:56	8:00	20:23	1:59	14:20	8:24	20:46	3:55	16:14	9:07	21:31	3:30	15:53	10:14	22:42	4:22	16:45	-----
9:10	21:30	8:38	20:58	2:37	14:57	9:00	21:20	4:30	16:48	9:47	22:08	4:12	16:34	10:52	23:14	5:00	17:21	-----
9:49	22:06	9:17	21:35	3:13	15:33	9:39	21:56	5:02	17:21	10:28	22:47	4:52	17:14	11:31	23:46	5:37	17:58	----
10:26	22:40	9:56	22:10	3:51	16:08	10:16	22:30	5:37	17:53	11:09	23:24	5:34	17:53	NT	12:12	6:16	18:34	---
11:05	**23:18**	**10:36**	**22:49**	**4:29**	**16:46**	**10:55**	**23:08**	**6:12**	**18:28**	**11:52**	**NT**	**6:16**	**18:35**	**0:16**	**12:59**	**6:57**	**19:14**	--
11:54	NT	11:26	23:39	5:13	17:32	11:44	23:56	6:53	19:10	0:05	12:45	7:04	19:27	0:51	14:03	7:50	20:07	
0:06	12:58	NT	12:32	6:11	18:35	NT	12:48	7:47	20:08	0:58	13:55	8:08	20:36	1:41	15:28	8:59	21:20	
1:08	14:25	0:42	13:59	7:26	20:02	0:58	14:15	8:56	21:36	2:06	15:21	9:31	22:03	2:44	16:57	10:17	22:48	
2:36	15:56	2:09	15:27	8:54	21:30	2:26	15:46	10:32	23:11	3:30	16:44	10:49	23:21	4:03	18:04	11:30	23:59	
3:58	16:57	3:29	16:26	10:03	22:28	3:48	16:47	11:47	NT	4:46	17:40	11:50	NT	5:12	18:50	NT	12:26	BST
4:54	17:42	4:24	17:10	10:52	23:13	4:44	17:32	0:14	12:40	5:38	18:22	0:13	12:33	6:07	19:28	0:48	13:11	-
4:39	17:18	4:09	16:47	10:34	22:52	4:29	17:08	23:33	12:21	5:24	18:00	23:52	12:17	5:57	19:03	0:31	12:53	GMT
5:20	17:52	4:49	17:20	11:12	23:27	5:10	17:42	0:40	13:02	6:02	18:31	0:33	12:51	6:43	19:37	1:09	13:31	---

NOVEMBER 2005

"NT" = No Tide

Times GMT

		Heights at CROMER				CROMER SHERINGHAM				KING'S LYNN QUAY				HUNSTANTON				BLAKENEY BAR			
		HIGH		LOW		HIGH WATER		LOW WATER		HIGH WATER		LOW WATER		HIGH WATER		LOW WATER		HIGH WATER		LOW WATER	
		AM	PM	AM	PM	AM	PM	AM	PM	AM	PM	AM	PM	AM	PM	AM	PM	AM	PM	AM	PM
1	TUES	4.7	4.7		1.0	5:42	18:08	0:08	12:27	5:36	18:03	0:49	13:57	5:23	17:51	NT	12:22	5:34	18:00	11:59	NT
2	WED	4.9	4.9	0.8	0.6	6:16	18:39	0:40	12:58	6:12	18:36	2:16	14:44	6:00	18:25	0:39	13:01	6:09	18:32	0:13	12:3
3	THUR	5.0	4.9	0.8	0.6	6:50	19:11	1:11	13:29	6:48	19:10	3:03	15:27	6:37	19:00	1:18	13:40	6:44	19:05	0:48	13:0
4	FRI	5.0	4.9	0.8	0.7	7:26	19:47	1:44	14:06	7:26	19:46	3:43	15:59	7:16	19:35	1:59	14:17	7:21	19:42	1:24	13:4
5	SAT	4.9	4.8	0.8	0.9	8:07	20:27	2:28	14:50	8:06	20:24	4:12	16:28	7:55	20:12	2:31	14:49	8:02	20:21	2:03	14:2
6	SUN	4.7	4.7	0.8	1.1	8:54	21:12	3:13	15:36	8:50	21:07	4:44	17:00	8:37	20:54	3:08	15:27	8:48	21:05	2:45	15:0
7	MON	4.5	4.5	1.0	1.4	9:48	22:04	4:07	16:27	9:41	21:56	5:20	17:36	9:27	21:42	3:50	16:10	9:40	21:55	3:35	15:5
8	TUES	4.2	4.3	1.2	1.8	10:52	23:07	5:06	17:34	10:42	22:56	6:02	18:21	10:26	22:40	4:41	17:01	10:43	22:57	4:31	16:5
9	WED		4.1	1.4	2.0	NT	12:11	6:22	18:52	11:56	NT	6:54	19:16	11:38	23:51	5:41	18:07	11:59	NT	5:41	18:1
10	THUR	4.1	4.0	1.4	2.0	0:26	13:41	7:49	20:27	0:10	13:21	7:53	20:23	NT	13:01	6:52	19:22	0:14	13:26	7:02	19:3
11	FRI	4.2	4.1	1.4	1.9	1:52	14:55	9:10	21:37	1:33	14:39	9:21	21:59	1:13	14:21	8:13	20:48	1:38	14:42	8:22	20:5
12	SAT	4.3	4.3	1.1	1.6	3:01	15:52	10:09	22:33	2:46	15:40	10:44	23:16	2:28	15:24	9:28	21:56	2:49	15:41	9:28	21:5
13	SUN	4.5	4.5	0.9	1.3	3:59	16:39	10:58	23:19	3:47	16:30	11:52	NT	3:31	16:15	10:29	22:54	3:48	16:30	10:21	22:4
14	MON	4.7	4.7	0.7	1.1	4:48	17:21	11:40	0:00	4:39	17:14	0:20	12:51	4:25	17:00	11:23	23:47	4:38	17:13	11:08	23:2
15	TUES	4.9	4.9		0.8	5:32	17:59	NT	12:20	5:26	17:54	1:19	13:46	5:13	17:42	NT	12:11	5:24	17:51	11:50	NT
16	WED	4.9	4.9	0.6	0.8	6:12	18:35	0:35	12:53	6:08	18:32	2:10	14:35	5:56	18:21	0:34	12:56	6:05	18:28	0:09	12:2
17	THUR	4.9	4.9	0.8	0.8	6:50	19:09	1:10	13:27	6:48	19:08	3:02	15:25	6:37	18:58	1:17	13:38	6:44	19:03	0:47	13:0
18	FRI	4.8	4.8	0.8	0.9	7:27	19:44	1:45	14:04	7:27	19:44	3:44	15:57	7:17	19:33	2:00	14:15	7:22	19:40	1:25	13:4
19	SAT	4.7	4.7	0.9	1.1	8:07	20:21	2:28	14:43	8:06	20:19	4:12	16:24	7:55	20:07	2:31	14:46	8:02	20:16	2:03	14:1
20	SUN	4.5	4.5	1.1	1.4	8:49	20:59	3:07	15:23	8:45	20:55	4:41	16:51	8:33	20:42	3:06	15:18	8:42	20:53	2:41	14:5
21	MON	4.2	4.3	1.2	1.7	9:33	21:43	3:53	16:08	9:27	21:36	5:11	17:21	9:14	21:22	3:40	15:51	9:25	21:35	3:22	15:3
22	TUES	4.0	4.1	1.4	2.0	10:24	22:29	4:41	16:56	10:15	22:20	5:45	17:55	10:00	22:05	4:20	16:31	10:15	22:20	4:08	16:2
23	WED	3.8	3.9	1.7	2.2	11:23	23:27	5:38	17:55	11:11	23:15	6:24	18:35	10:55	22:58	5:05	17:18	11:12	23:17	5:00	17:1
24	THUR		3.9	1.8	2.3	NT	12:33	6:44	19:05	NT	12:17	7:09	19:22	11:58	23:58	5:59	18:16	NT	12:21	6:02	18:2
25	FRI	3.7	3.7	1.8	2.3	0:33	13:48	7:59	20:08	0:17	13:29	7:59	20:22	NT	13:09	6:58	19:21	0:21	13:34	7:11	19:3
26	SAT	3.9	3.8	1.7	2.2	1:48	14:51	9:05	21:28	1:29	14:35	9:15	21:46	1:09	14:17	8:08	20:35	1:34	14:38	8:18	20:4
27	SUN	4.0	4.0	1.6	2.0	2:49	15:40	9:57	22:16	2:33	15:27	10:27	22:53	2:15	15:11	9:12	21:35	2:36	15:28	9:14	21:3
28	MON	4.1	4.2	1.4	1.7	3:41	16:22	10:41	22:59	3:28	16:12	11:29	23:53	3:12	15:57	10:08	22:30	3:29	16:12	10:03	22:2
29	TUES	4.4	4.4	1.1	1.4	4:27	17:00	11:21	23:38	4:17	16:52	NT	12:23	4:02	16:38	10:56	23:17	4:17	16:51	10:45	23:04
30	WED	4.6	4.6	1.0		5:09	17:37	11:57	NT	5:01	17:31	0:46	13:15	4:47	17:18	11:44	NT	5:00	17:29	11:26	23:4

NOVEMBER 2005

"NT" = No Tide

BURNHAM Overy Staithe		WELLS BAR				WELLS QUAY				HEMSBY				Gt.YARMOUTH Britannia Pier				
HIGH WATER		HIGH WATER		LOW WATER		HIGH WATER		LOW WATER		HIGH WATER		LOW WATER		HIGH WATER		LOW WATER		
AM	PM	AM	PM	AM	PM	AM	PM	AM	PM	AM	PM	AM	PM	AM	PM	AM	PM	
5:58	18:26	5:26	17:53	11:47	NT	5:48	18:16	1:18	13:40	6:37	19:03	0:55	13:22	7:26	20:10	1:45	14:07	----
6:35	19:00	6:02	18:26	0:02	12:22	6:25	18:50	1:57	14:18	7:11	19:34	1:35	13:53	8:08	20:43	2:22	14:44	-----
7:12	19:35	6:38	19:00	0:37	12:57	7:02	19:25	2:34	14:56	7:45	20:06	2:06	14:24	8:48	21:16	2:58	15:20	-----
7:51	20:10	7:16	19:36	1:14	13:34	7:41	20:00	3:14	15:32	8:21	20:42	2:39	15:01	9:30	21:51	3:36	15:58	-----
8:30	20:47	7:56	20:14	1:52	14:12	8:20	20:37	3:48	16:06	9:02	21:22	3:23	15:45	10:13	22:26	4:16	16:37	-----
9:12	21:29	8:40	20:57	2:33	14:54	9:02	21:19	4:26	16:45	9:49	22:07	4:08	16:31	11:02	23:04	5:00	17:20	----
10:02	22:17	9:31	21:46	3:21	15:41	9:52	22:07	5:09	17:29	10:43	22:59	5:02	17:22	11:58	23:49	5:52	18:11	---
11:01	23:15	10:32	22:46	4:16	16:40	10:51	23:05	6:01	18:22	11:47	NT	6:01	18:29	NT	13:13	6:54	19:14	--
NT	12:13	11:46	23:55	5:24	17:52	NT	12:03	7:03	19:29	0:20	13:06	7:17	19:47	0:46	14:37	8:07	20:31	--
0:26	13:36	NT	13:11	6:43	19:17	0:16	13:26	8:16	20:47	1:21	14:36	8:44	21:22	1:56	15:59	9:25	21:54	-
1:48	14:56	1:23	14:29	8:04	20:35	1:38	14:46	9:38	22:11	2:47	15:50	10:05	22:32	3:16	17:04	10:37	23:04	--
3:03	15:59	2:36	15:30	9:11	21:37	2:53	15:49	10:50	23:18	3:56	16:47	11:04	23:28	4:30	17:57	11:38	NT	--
4:06	16:50	3:37	16:20	10:06	22:29	3:56	16:40	11:50	NT	4:54	17:34	11:53	NT	5:36	18:43	0:02	12:31	---
5:00	17:35	4:29	17:04	10:54	23:16	4:50	17:25	0:15	12:42	5:43	18:16	0:14	12:35	6:33	19:25	0:53	13:18	----
5:48	18:17	5:16	17:44	11:38	23:57	5:38	18:07	1:06	13:30	6:27	18:54	0:55	13:15	7:23	20:03	1:38	14:00	-----
6:31	18:56	5:58	18:22	NT	12:17	6:21	18:46	1:51	14:13	7:07	19:30	1:30	13:48	8:08	20:38	2:19	14:40	-----
7:12	19:33	6:38	18:58	0:36	12:55	7:02	19:23	2:33	14:54	7:45	20:04	2:05	14:22	8:51	21:12	2:59	15:18	-----
7:52	20:08	7:17	19:34	1:15	13:32	7:42	19:58	3:15	15:30	8:22	20:39	2:40	14:59	9:32	21:44	3:38	15:54	-----
8:30	20:42	7:56	20:09	1:52	14:07	8:20	20:32	3:48	16:02	9:02	21:16	3:23	15:38	10:12	22:14	4:16	16:29	---
9:08	21:17	8:35	20:45	2:29	14:43	8:58	21:07	4:23	16:35	9:44	21:54	4:02	16:18	10:55	22:45	4:55	17:05	---
9:49	21:57	9:17	21:26	3:09	15:22	9:39	21:47	4:59	17:10	10:28	22:38	4:48	17:03	11:43	23:21	5:38	17:45	--
10:35	22:40	10:05	22:10	3:53	16:06	10:25	22:30	5:39	17:51	11:19	23:24	5:36	17:51	NT	12:41	6:28	18:30	-
11:30	23:33	11:01	23:05	4:44	16:59	11:20	23:23	6:26	18:40	NT	12:18	6:33	18:50	0:02	13:50	7:25	19:28	-
NT	12:33	NT	12:07	5:44	18:03	NT	12:23	7:21	19:39	0:22	13:28	7:39	20:00	0:55	15:02	8:28	20:36	
0:33	13:44	0:07	13:19	6:51	19:16	0:23	13:34	8:22	20:46	1:28	14:43	8:54	21:21	1:55	16:08	9:31	21:48	
1:44	14:52	1:19	14:25	7:59	20:24	1:34	14:42	9:32	21:59	2:43	15:46	10:00	22:23	3:03	17:01	10:31	22:50	
2:50	15:46	2:23	15:17	8:57	21:18	2:40	15:36	10:35	22:58	3:44	16:35	10:52	23:11	4:07	17:43	11:22	23:40	-
3:47	16:32	3:18	16:02	9:47	22:07	3:37	16:22	11:29	23:51	4:36	17:17	11:36	23:54	5:06	18:23	NT	12:10	--
4:37	17:13	4:07	16:42	10:31	22:50	4:27	17:03	NT	12:17	5:22	17:55	NT	12:16	6:02	19:00	0:28	12:53	---
5:22	17:53	4:51	17:21	11:13	23:33	5:12	17:43	0:37	13:03	6:04	18:32	0:33	12:52	6:54	19:38	1:11	13:35	----

DECEMBER 2005

"NT" = No Tide

Times GMT

		Heights at CROMER				CROMER SHERINGHAM				KING'S LYNN QUAY				HUNSTANTON				BLAKENEY BAR			
		HIGH		LOW		HIGH WATER		LOW WATER		HIGH WATER		LOW WATER		HIGH WATER		LOW WATER		HIGH WATER		LOW WATER	
		AM	PM	AM	PM	AM	PM	AM	PM	AM	PM	AM	PM	AM	PM	AM	PM	AM	PM	AM	PM
1	THUR	4.7	4.8	0.8	0.9	5:50	18:13	0:15	12:32	5:45	18:09	1:40	14:06	5:32	17:57	0:06	12:31	5:43	18:06	NT	12:0
2	FRI	4.9	4.9	0.8	0.8	6:31	18:51	0:50	13:09	6:28	18:49	2:31	15:00	6:17	18:38	0:53	13:16	6:24	18:45	0:25	12:4
3	SAT	4.9	4.9	0.7	0.8	7:14	19:31	1:30	13:50	7:13	19:31	3:28	15:46	7:03	19:21	1:41	14:01	7:08	19:26	1:08	13:2
4	SUN	4.9	4.9	0.6	0.9	8:00	20:16	2:17	14:38	7:59	20:14	4:06	16:20	7:48	20:02	2:24	14:41	7:55	20:11	1:54	14:1
5	MON	4.7	4.9	0.6	1.1	8:51	21:05	3:07	15:30	8:47	21:01	4:41	16:55	8:34	20:48	3:06	15:21	8:45	20:59	2:41	15:0
6	TUES	4.5	4.7	0.8	1.4	9:47	22:00	4:03	16:23	9:40	21:52	5:19	17:33	9:26	21:38	3:50	16:06	9:39	21:51	3:33	15:5
7	WED	4.3	4.5	0.9	1.6	10:48	23:00	5:05	17:26	10:38	22:49	6:02	18:16	10:22	22:33	4:40	16:57	10:39	22:50	4:30	16:5
8	THUR	4.2		1.1	1.7	11:57	NT	6:14	18:36	11:43	23:52	6:48	19:03	11:26	23:34	5:33	17:51	11:45	23:55	5:33	17:5
9	FRI	4.4	4.1	1.2	1.9	0:07	13:12	7:25	19:55	NT	12:53	7:36	19:56	NT	12:34	6:32	18:54	NT	12:57	6:40	19:0
10	SAT	4.3	4.1	1.3	1.8	1:23	14:20	8:42	21:04	1:04	14:03	8:42	21:14	0:44	13:44	7:37	20:07	1:09	14:07	7:51	20:1
11	SUN	4.3	4.2	1.3	1.7	2:29	15:20	9:39	22:05	2:12	15:06	10:02	22:37	1:54	14:49	8:50	21:20	2:15	15:08	8:54	21:2
12	MON	4.3	4.3	1.2	1.5	3:31	16:13	10:33	22:55	3:18	16:02	11:16	23:48	3:01	15:47	9:56	22:26	3:20	16:02	9:53	22:1
13	TUES	4.5	4.5	1.1	1.4	4:25	16:58	11:19	23:39	4:15	16:50	NT	12:20	4:00	16:36	10:54	23:22	4:15	16:49	10:43	23:0
14	WED	4.5	4.6	1.1		5:13	17:39	11:59	NT	5:05	17:33	0:50	13:17	4:51	17:20	11:46	NT	5:04	17:31	11:28	23:5
15	THUR	4.6	4.7	1.1	1.1	5:56	18:17	0:20	12:35	5:51	18:13	1:46	14:10	5:39	18:01	0:11	12:34	5:48	18:10	NT	12:0
16	FRI	4.6	4.7	1.1	1.1	6:36	18:52	0:56	13:11	6:33	18:50	2:42	15:03	6:22	18:39	0:59	13:18	6:29	18:46	0:31	12:4
17	SAT	4.6	4.7	1.1	1.2	7:14	19:27	1:31	13:44	7:13	19:27	3:29	15:43	7:03	19:17	1:42	13:59	7:08	19:22	1:09	13:2
18	SUN	4.6	4.7	1.0	1.3	7:53	20:04	2:12	14:25	7:52	20:03	4:02	16:12	7:41	19:52	2:19	14:32	7:48	19:59	1:49	14:0.
19	MON	4.4	4.6	1.0	1.4	8:35	20:43	2:54	15:06	8:32	20:40	4:31	16:40	8:20	20:28	2:53	15:05	8:29	20:37	2:28	14:4(
20	TUES	4.3	4.5	1.1	1.6	9:17	21:22	3:37	15:49	9:12	21:17	5:01	17:08	8:59	21:04	3:28	15:36	9:10	21:15	3:08	15:1
21	WED	4.1	4.4	1.2	1.7	10:01	22:04	4:21	16:31	9:53	21:56	5:31	17:37	9:39	21:42	4:04	16:10	9:52	21:55	3:49	15:5
22	THUR	4.0	4.3	1.4	1.9	10:46	22:47	5:06	17:15	10:36	22:37	6:02	18:08	10:20	22:21	4:41	16:46	10:37	22:38	4:31	16:3
23	FRI	3.9	4.1	1.5	2.0	11:37	23:38	5:56	18:06	11:24	23:25	6:36	18:44	11:07	23:08	5:19	17:29	11:26	23:27	5:16	17:2
24	SAT		4.0	1.6	2.1	NT	12:35	6:52	19:07	NT	12:19	7:16	19:24	NT	12:00	6:07	18:18	NT	12:23	6:10	18:2
25	SUN	4.1	3.8	1.7	2.2	0:37	13:39	7:57	20:17	0:21	13:19	7:57	20:12	0:02	12:59	6:56	19:12	0:25	13:24	7:09	19:2
26	MON	4.0	3.9	1.7	2.0	1:43	14:37	8:59	21:19	1:23	14:21	9:05	21:32	1:03	14:03	7:58	20:22	1:28	14:24	8:10	20:3
27	TUES	4.1	4.0	1.6	1.9	2:45	15:33	9:53	22:16	2:29	15:20	10:22	22:53	2:11	15:03	9:08	21:35	2:32	15:22	9:10	21:3
28	WED	4.2	4.2	1.4	1.6	3:45	16:24	10:45	23:08	3:33	16:14	11:33	NT	3:17	15:59	10:12	22:39	3:34	16:14	10:07	22:3
29	THUR	4.4	4.5	1.2	1.2	4:41	17:11	11:32	23:53	4:32	17:03	0:04	12:39	4:17	16:49	11:11	23:40	4:32	17:02	10:58	23:2
30	FRI	4.6	4.7		0.8	5:32	17:55	NT	12:16	5:26	17:50	1:10	13:41	5:13	17:38	NT	12:07	5:24	17:47	11:47	NT
31	SAT	4.8	4.9	1.1	0.9	6:21	18:40	0:39	12:57	6:17	18:37	2:15	14:46	6:05	18:26	0:38	13:04	6:14	18:33	0:12	12:34

DECEMBER 2005

"NT" = No Tide

BURNHAM OVERY STAITHE		WELLS BAR				WELLS QUAY				HEMSBY				Gt.YARMOUTH BRITANNIA PIER				
HIGH WATER		HIGH WATER		LOW WATER		HIGH WATER		LOW WATER		HIGH WATER		LOW WATER		HIGH WATER		LOW WATER		
AM	PM	AM	PM	AM	PM	AM	PM	AM	PM	AM	PM	AM	PM	AM	PM	AM	PM	
6:07	18:32	5:35	17:59	11:54	NT	5:57	18:22	1:24	13:48	6:45	19:08	1:10	13:27	7:44	20:15	1:55	14:17	-----
6:52	19:13	6:18	18:39	0:14	12:35	6:42	19:03	2:10	14:32	7:26	19:46	1:45	14:04	8:32	20:54	2:38	14:59	-----
7:38	19:56	7:03	19:21	0:58	13:18	7:28	19:56	2:57	15:17	8:09	20:26	2:25	14:45	9:22	21:34	3:23	15:43	-----
8:23	20:37	7:49	20:04	1:43	14:02	8:13	20:27	3:40	15:57	8:55	21:11	3:12	15:33	10:12	22:15	4:10	16:27	-----
9:09	21:23	8:37	20:51	2:29	14:48	8:59	21:13	4:23	16:39	9:46	22:00	4:02	16:25	11:05	22:57	4:59	17:14	-----
10:01	22:13	9:30	21:42	3:19	15:37	9:51	22:03	5:08	17:25	10:42	22:55	4:58	17:18	11:59	23:43	5:52	18:05	---
10:57	23:08	10:28	22:39	4:15	16:34	10:47	22:58	6:00	18:17	11:43	23:55	6:00	18:21	NT	13:08	6:51	19:03	---
NT	12:01	11:33	23:42	5:16	17:36	11:51	23:59	6:55	19:14	NT	12:52	7:09	19:31	0:36	14:17	7:54	20:07	---
0:09	13:09	NT	12:43	6:21	18:47	NT	12:59	7:55	20:19	1:02	14:07	8:20	20:50	1:37	15:28	9:01	21:21	-
1:19	14:19	0:54	13:53	7:32	19:58	1:09	14:09	9:03	21:31	2:18	15:15	9:37	21:59	2:47	16:31	10:07	22:28	--
2:29	15:24	2:02	14:56	8:37	21:05	2:19	15:14	10:14	22:43	3:24	16:15	10:34	23:00	3:58	17:27	11:08	23:33	--
3:36	16:22	3:08	15:52	9:37	22:03	3:26	16:12	11:18	23:47	4:26	17:08	11:28	23:50	5:07	18:15	NT	12:04	--
4:35	17:11	4:05	16:40	10:29	22:53	4:25	17:01	NT	12:15	5:20	17:53	NT	12:14	6:08	18:58	0:28	12:53	--
5:26	17:55	4:55	17:23	11:15	23:38	5:16	17:45	0:41	13:05	6:08	18:34	0:34	12:54	7:01	19:37	1:16	13:37	----
6:14	18:36	5:41	18:03	11:57	NT	6:04	18:26	1:30	13:51	6:51	19:12	1:15	13:30	7:51	20:14	2:01	14:19	----
6:57	19:14	6:23	18:40	0:20	12:37	6:47	19:04	2:16	14:34	7:31	19:47	1:51	14:06	8:36	20:49	2:43	14:57	----
7:38	19:52	7:03	19:17	0:59	13:14	7:28	19:42	2:58	15:14	8:09	20:22	2:26	14:39	9:18	21:22	3:23	15:34	---
8:16	20:27	7:42	19:53	1:38	13:51	8:06	20:17	3:35	15:48	8:48	20:59	3:07	15:20	10:00	21:55	4:02	16:10	----
8:55	21:03	8:22	20:30	2:16	14:28	8:45	20:53	4:10	16:22	9:30	21:38	3:49	16:01	10:43	22:27	4:42	16:47	---
9:34	21:39	9:02	21:07	2:55	15:05	9:24	21:29	4:46	16:55	10:12	22:17	4:32	16:44	11:26	23:01	5:22	17:23	---
10:14	22:17	9:43	21:46	3:35	15:43	10:04	22:07	5:23	17:30	10:56	22:59	5:16	17:26	12:00	23:36	6:04	18:01	---
10:55	22:56	10:26	22:27	4:16	16:23	10:45	22:46	6:01	18:07	11:41	23:42	6:01	18:10	NT	13:01	6:49	18:42	--
11:42	23:43	11:14	23:15	5:00	17:10	11:32	23:33	6:41	18:50	NT	12:32	6:51	19:01	0:15	13:56	7:37	19:32	--
NT	12:35	NT	12:09	5:52	18:05	NT	12:25	7:29	19:41	0:33	13:30	7:47	20:02	1:04	14:55	8:32	20:31	-
0:37	13:34	0:11	13:09	6:49	19:07	0:27	13:24	8:20	20:37	1:32	14:34	8:52	21:12	2:00	15:53	9:29	21:35	
1:38	14:38	1:13	14:11	7:51	20:13	1:28	14:28	9:23	21:47	2:38	15:32	9:54	22:14	3:05	16:48	10:27	22:42	
2:46	15:38	2:19	15:10	8:53	21:18	2:36	15:28	10:31	22:58	3:40	16:28	10:48	23:11	4:15	17:37	11:24	23:45	-
3:52	16:34	3:23	16:04	9:51	22:16	3:42	16:24	11:33	0:00	4:40	17:19	11:40	NT	5:25	18:24	NT	12:19	--
4:52	17:24	4:22	16:53	10:44	23:09	4:42	17:14	NT	12:31	5:36	18:06	0:03	12:27	6:30	19:09	0:42	13:09	---
5:48	18:13	5:16	17:40	11:34	NT	5:38	18:03	0:59	13:25	6:27	18:50	0:48	13:11	7:30	19:55	1:34	13:59	----
6:40	19:01	6:07	18:27	0:01	12:23	6:30	18:51	1:56	14:20	7:16	19:35	1:34	13:52	8:27	20:40	2:26	14:48	-----

SAFETY NOTES

Most lifeboat call outs to motor boats are for mechanical breakdowns. Engines should be regularly maintained. All craft should carry life jackets and harnesses, spare fuel, first aid kit, warm clothing, communication equipment and up to date charts.

Always carry oars or spare outboard motor.

Many of our river estuaries have complicated tidal flows. Walkers unfamiliar with the area should not cross to the seaward side of channels. **Return to dry land several hours before the next high tide.**

Inflatable beach toys and sailboards should be used with extreme caution. These are responsible for the largest number of call outs.

PLEASE closely supervise young children at all times.

When walking the coast line, plan your route and keep someone informed of your intentions. If on holiday tell your Hotel / B&B, they can notify the authorities if you are in trouble. Carry a mobile phone but check network coverage regularly. Remember to keep your contact informed of any delay.

The East Anglian coastline is constantly subjected to erosion due to the strong winds and tidal currents of the North Sea resulting in undercut and unstable cliffs. It is dangerous to dig into or climb the cliffs. Care should be taken when using cliff top walks. Some paths may be closed for safety reasons. Please do not leave litter. In particular drink cans, plastic bags, fishing nets and line are hazardous to wildlife.

BURNHAM OVERY BOATHOUSE

Chandlery
Liesureware
Gifts
Boat Maintenance

Tel: 01328 738348
Fax:01328 730550

BURNHAM OVERY BOATHOUSE LTD.
THE QUAY
BURNHAM OVERY STAITHE.
NORFOLK NR31 8JF